Basics of Human Behavior

Absorbing, easy to read and understand, here is a fascinating presentation of Freud's principal theories on psychology. Culled from forty years of writing by the founder of psychoanalysis, this is the *first* book which gives, in a comprehensive and systematic form, Freud's thinking on the organization, dynamics and development of the normal human personality.

Calvin S. Hall outlines Freud's penetrating diagnosis of the balances existing between the mind and emotions, and points out his important discoveries about the parts played by instincts, the conscious and unconscious, and anxiety in the functioning of the human psyche. In discussing the elements that form personality, the author explains the ideas of the pioneer thinker in psychology on defense mechanisms, the channeling of instinctual drives, and the role of sex in the boy and girl maturing into man and woman.

Lucid, illuminating and instructive, this is an important book for everyone who wants to understand human behavior—in himself and in others.

"A Primer of Freudian Psychology is compact, readable, accurate."
—Gordon W. Allport, Professor of Psychology,
Harvard University

CALVIN S. HALL, Senior Lecturer in Psychology and Fellow of Cowell College, University of California, Santa Cruz, is also author or co-author of a number of other books, including *THE CONTENT ANALYSIS OF DREAMS, THEORIES OF PERSONALITY, THE INDIVIDUAL AND HIS DREAMS,* and *A PRIMER OF JUNGIAN PSYCHOLOGY.*

Other MENTOR Books of Special Interest

A PRIMER OF
Freudian Psychology

By CALVIN S. HALL
Professor of Psychology
Western Reserve University

A MENTOR BOOK from
NEW AMERICAN LIBRARY
TIMES MIRROR
New York and Scarborough, Ontario
The New English Library Limited, London

MENTOR TRADEMARK REG. U.S. PAT. OFF. AND FOREIGN COUNTRIES
REGISTERED TRADEMARK—MARCA REGISTRADA
HECHO EN CHICAGO, U.S.A.

SIGNET, SIGNET CLASSICS, MENTOR, PLUME AND MERIDIAN BOOKS
are published *in the United States* by
The New American Library, Inc.,
1301 Avenue of the Americas, New York, New York 10019,
in Canada by The New American Library of Canada Limited,
81 Mack Avenue, Scarborough, 704, Ontario,
in the United Kingdom by The New English Library Limited,
Barnard's Inn, Holborn, London, E.C. 1, England.

25 26 27 28 29 30 31 32 33

PRINTED IN THE UNITED STATES OF AMERICA

THIS PRIMER IS DEDICATED TO
MY STUDENTS, WHO HELPED TO WRITE IT,
AND TO THE MEMORY OF SIGMUND FREUD,
WHO FURNISHED THE IDEAS.

Preface

MY REASON for writing this primer is to present as clearly, as briefly, and as systematically as I can the psychological theories advanced by Sigmund Freud.

Freud's contributions in the areas of abnormal psychology, psychopathology, psychotherapy, and psychiatry have been summarized by a number of writers, but his work as a psychological theorist in the area of general psychology has not been presented in a systematic and comprehensive form as far as I have been able to discover.

In my opinion, which is shared I believe by an increasing number of fellow psychologists, Freud's distinctive role in intellectual and scientific history is that of a psychological theorist. Freud himself regarded psychoanalysis primarily as a system of psychology and not merely a branch of abnormal psychology or psychiatry. He wanted to be remembered and identified chiefly as a psychologist.

My purpose then in summarizing the psychology of Sigmund Freud is to rescue him from the domain of mental disorders and to restore him to his legitimate place within the province of normal psychology. In stating my purpose in this way I do not intend any disparagement of Freud's considerable contributions to psychiatry. These contributions by themselves would assure him a secure place in history. However, I feel that if Freud is permitted to remain an exclusive possession of a branch of medicine, not only will his fundamental theories be relegated to a subordinate position, but also psychology will be the loser for having ignored one of its most creative minds.

This primer is purely expository. I have not attempted to evaluate or criticize Freud's theories or to examine them in comparison with other theories, because I feel that one should thoroughly understand something before his criticisms will be of much value. One is dismayed by the prevalence of criticism based upon incomplete understanding. Freud seems to have suffered more, in this respect, than any other major thinker of our times. His theories have been so widely misrepresented and distorted that it is almost impossible for the unsuspecting reader to separate fact from falsification.

The exposition of Freud's psychology is not an easy one. His ideas are scattered throughout his writings from the early 1890's to the late 1930's, and one has to read everything he wrote to be sure that no essential point is missed. Moreover, I was confronted with the task of making decisions regarding Freud's final views on a number of theoretical points, since I did not feel that this primer should be a historical account of Freud's ideas. Freud was continually revising, modifying, and expanding his theories. Some of his early views were discarded and many were reworded. In making these decisions I have tried to use all of the available evidence and my own judgment. Undoubtedly errors of judgment have been made. It is possible that I have "read into" Freud what I wanted to find there, but I have tried to avoid this mistake by keeping the possibility of making it in the forefront of my mind. When I felt that I might be reading into Freud something that is not there I went back to his writings for confirmation. I hope that the result is a "reading out" of Freud rather than a "reading into" Freud.

In writing the primer I have used only primary sources, namely, the published writings of Freud. I thought it better to abide by what Freud himself said than to depend upon secondary sources. Any reader can cover some of the same ground by reading the references given at the end of each chapter, and all of it by reading the collected works of Freud which happily are now being made available in a new standard edition in English.

This primer has been written for the general reader as well as for students in psychology classes. I have benefited greatly from the thoughtful and practical suggestions made by my students who read the primer in a preliminary draft. They helped me to express myself in ways that would be more comprehensible to the general reader whose background in psychology may be limited. I have tried to express my appreciation by dedicating the primer to them.

CALVIN S. HALL
Department of Psychology
Western Reserve University

Cleveland, Ohio
April, 1954

Contents

... a man like me cannot live without a hobby-horse, a consuming passion—in Schiller's words a tyrant. I have found my tyrant, and in his service I know no limits. My tyrant is psychology.

—FREUD, 1895
From a letter to Wilhelm Fliess

CHAPTER ONE

Sigmund Freud
(1856-1939)

I. FREUD'S SCIENTIFIC HERITAGE

Although Sigmund Freud was born in Freiberg, Moravia, and died in London, England, he belongs to Vienna, where he lived for nearly eighty years. Had the Nazis not taken over Austria in 1937, forcing Freud to seek haven in England, his whole life, except for the first three years of it, would have been spent in the Austrian capital.

Freud's long life, from 1856 to 1939, spans one of the most creative periods in the history of science. The same year that the three-year-old Freud was taken by his family to Vienna saw the publication of Charles Darwin's *Origin of Species*. This book was destined to revolutionize man's conception of man. Before Darwin, man was set apart from the rest of the animal kingdom by virtue of his having a soul. The evolutionary doctrine made man a part of nature, an animal among other animals. The acceptance of this radical view meant that the study of man could proceed along naturalistic lines. Man became an object of scientific study, no different, save in complexity, from other forms of life.

The year following the publication of the *Origin of Species*, when Freud was four years old, Gustav Fechner founded the science of psychology. This great German scientist and philosopher of the nineteenth century demonstrated in 1860 that mind could be studied scientifically and that it could be measured quantitatively. Psychology took its place among the other natural sciences.

These two men, Darwin and Fechner, had a tremendous impact upon the intellectual development of Freud as they did upon so many other young men of that period. Interest in the biological sciences and psychology flourished during the second half of the nineteenth century. Louis Pasteur and Robert Koch, by their fundamental work on the germ theory of disease, established the science of bacteriology; and Gregor Mendel, by his investigations on the garden pea, founded the modern science of genetics. The life sciences were on a creative rampage.

There were other influences that affected Freud even more profoundly. These came from physics. In the middle of the century, the great German physicist, Hermann von Helmholtz, formulated the principle of the conservation of energy. This principle stated, in effect, that energy is a quantity just as mass is a quantity. It can be transformed but it cannot be destroyed. When energy disappears from one part of a system it has to appear elsewhere in the system. For example, as one object becomes cooler an adjacent object becomes warmer.

The study of energy changes in a physical system led to one momentous discovery after another in the field of dynamics. The fifty years between Helmholtz's statement of the conservation of energy and Albert Einstein's theory of relativity was the golden age of energy. Thermodynamics, the electromagnetic field, radioactivity, the electron, the quantum theory—these are some of the achievements of this vital half-century. Such men as James Maxwell, Heinrich Hertz, Max Planck, Sir Joseph Thomson, Marie and Pierre Curie, James Joule, Lord Kelvin, Josiah Gibbs, Rudolph Clausius, Dmitri Mendelyeev—to name only a few of the titans of modern physics—were literally changing the world by their discoveries of the secrets of energy. Most of the labor-saving devices that make our lives so much easier today flowed from the vast cornucopia of nineteenth-century physics. We are still reaping the benefits of this golden age, as the newly installed atomic age bears witness.

But the age of energy and dynamics did more than provide man with electrical appliances, television, automobiles, airplanes, and atomic and hydrogen bombs. It furnished him with a new conception of man. Darwin conceived of man as an animal. Fechner proved that the mind of man did not stand outside of science but that it could be brought into the laboratory and accurately measured. The new physics, however, made possible an even more radical view of man. This is the view that man is an energy system and that he obeys the same physical laws which regulate the soap bubble and the movement of the planets.

As a young scientist engaged in biological research during the last quarter of the nineteenth century, Freud could hardly avoid being influenced by the new physics. Energy and dynamics were seeping into every laboratory and permeating the minds of scientists. It was Freud's good fortune, as a medical student, to come under the influence of Ernst Brücke. Brücke was Director of the Physiology Laboratory at the University of Vienna and one of the greatest physiologists of the century. His book, *Lectures on Physiology*, published in 1874, the year after Freud entered medical school, set forth the radical view that the living organism is a dynamic system to which the laws of chemistry and physics apply. Freud greatly admired Brücke and quickly became indoctrinated by this new dynamic physiology.

Thanks to Freud's singular genius, he was to discover some twenty years later that the laws of dynamics could be applied to man's personality as well as to his body. When he made his discovery Freud proceeded to create a dynamic psychology. A dynamic psychology is one that studies the transformations and exchanges of energy within the personality. This was Freud's greatest achievement, and one of the greatest achievements in modern science. It is certainly the crucial event in the history of psychology.

II. FREUD CREATES A DYNAMIC PSYCHOLOGY

Although Freud was trained in medicine and received his medical degree from the University of Vienna in 1881, he never intended to practice medicine. He wanted to be a scientist.

In pursuit of this goal, he entered the medical school of the University of Vienna in 1873, when he was seventeen years old, and undertook his first original piece of research in 1876. In this initial investigation he was looking for the recondite testes of the eel! He found them. For about fifteen years thereafter Freud devoted himself to investigations of the nervous system. Not exclusively so, however, because he found that the financial rewards of scientific research would not support a wife, six children, and sundry relatives. Moreover, the anti-Semitism that prevailed in Vienna during this period prevented Freud from receiving university advancement. Consequently, much against his wishes and upon the advice of Brücke, he was forced to take up the practice of medicine. In spite of his practice, he found time for neurological research, and eventually earned a reputation as a promising young scientist.

In a way it was fortunate that Freud was forced to practice medicine. Had he remained a medical scientist he might never have created a dynamic psychology. Contact with patients stimulated him to think in psychological terms.

When Freud began the practice of medicine it was natural, in view of his scientific background, that he should specialize in the treatment of nervous disorders. This branch of medicine was in a backward state. There was not a great deal that could be done for people suffering from aberrations of the mind. Jean Charcot, in France, was having some success with hypnosis, particularly in the treatment of hysteria. Freud spent a year in Paris (1885-86) learning Charcot's method of treatment. However, Freud was not satisfied with hypnosis because he felt that its effects were only temporary and did not get at the seat of the trouble. From another Viennese physician, Joseph Breuer, he learned of the benefits of the cathartic or "talking-out-your-problems" form of therapy. The patient talked while the physician listened. Although Freud was later to develop new and improved therapeutic techniques, the "talking-out" or free-association method provided him with a great deal of knowledge about the underlying causes of abnormal behavior. With true scientific curiosity and zeal, he began to probe deeper and deeper into the minds of his patients. His probing revealed dynamic forces at work which were responsible for creating the abnormal symptoms that he was called upon to treat. Gradually there began to take shape in Freud's mind the idea that most of these forces are unconscious.

This was the turning point in Freud's scientific life. Putting physiology and neurology aside, he became a psychological investigator. The room in which he treated his patients became his laboratory, the couch his only piece of equipment, and the ramblings of his patients his scientific data. Add to these the restless, penetrating mind of Freud, and one has named all of the ingredients that went into the creation of a dynamic psychology.

In the 1890's, with characteristic thoroughness, Freud began an intensive self-analysis of his own unconscious forces in order to check on the material supplied by his patients. By analyzing his dreams and saying to himself whatever came into his mind, he was able to see the workings of his own inner dynamics. On the basis of the knowledge gained from his patients and from himself he began to lay the foundation for a theory of personality. The development of this theory engaged his most creative efforts for the rest of his life. Later, he was to write, "My life has been aimed at one goal only; to infer or to guess how the mental apparatus is constructed and what forces interplay and counteract in it."

It was during the nineties that *The Interpretation of Dreams* was written, although it was not published until the last days of the century and given the publication date 1900. It was an auspicious beginning for the new century. This book, which is now considered to be one of the great works of modern times, is more than a book about dreams. It is a book about the dynamics of the human mind. The last chapter, in particular, contains Freud's theory of the mind.

Few laymen read the book when it first appeared, and it was ignored in medical and scientific circles. It took eight years to sell the first printing of six hundred copies. But the initial failure of *The Interpretation of Dreams* did not faze Freud. With the confidence of a man who knows that he is on the right track, Freud continued to explore man's mind by the method of psychoanalysis. At the same time that he was helping his patients to overcome their troubles, they were helping him to extend his knowledge of unconscious forces.

In spite of the poor reception accorded *The Interpretation of Dreams*, a succession of brilliant books and articles flowed from Freud's pen during the next ten years. In 1904, he published *The Psychopathology of Everyday Life*, which presented the novel thesis that slips of the tongue, errors, accidents, and faulty memory are all due to unconscious motives. The following year three more significant works appeared. One of these, *A Case of Hysteria*, gave a detailed account of Freud's method of tracking down the psychological causes of mental disorders. *Three Essays on Sexuality* set forth Freud's views on the development of the sex instinct. By many authorities this is considered to be Freud's most important work aside from *The Interpretation of Dreams*. Whether one agrees with this evaluation or not—and the present writer does not—the *Three Essays* earned for Freud the unwarranted reputation of being a pan-sexualist. The third volume, *Wit and Its Relation to the Unconscious*, showed how the jokes that people tell are the product of unconscious mechanisms.

Although, for a number of years, Freud worked pretty much in isolation from the rest of the scientific and medical world, his writings and the success of the psychoanalytic method in treating neurotic patients brought his name to the attention of a small group of people. Among these were Carl Jung and Alfred Adler, both of whom were later to withdraw their support of psychoanalysis and develop rival schools. But they were important followers of Freud in the years before the First

World War and helped to establish psychoanalysis as an international movement.

In 1909, Freud received his first academic recognition by being invited to speak at the twentieth anniversary celebration of the founding of Clark University in Worcester, Massachusetts. Stanley Hall, the president of Clark University and himself a distinguished psychologist, recognized the importance of Freud's contribution to psychology and helped to promote his views in the United States.

More and more recognition came to Freud, and following the First World War his name became known to millions of people throughout the world. Psychoanalysis was the rage, and its influence was felt in every theater of life. Literature, art, religion, social customs, morals, ethics, education, the social sciences—all felt the impact of Freudian psychology. It was considered fashionable to be psychoanalyzed and to use such words as subconscious, repressed urges, inhibitions, complexes, and fixations in one's conversation. Much of the popular interest in psychoanalysis was due to its association with sex.

Throughout his life Freud continued to write. Hardly a year passed when he did not publish at least one important book or article. His collected works, which are now appearing in a standard English edition, will fill twenty-four volumes. Freud is said to have been a master of prose writing. He had a felicity of expression that is unequaled among scientific writers. Without talking down to his readers, he nevertheless managed to convey his ideas in a lively, interesting, and lucid form.

Freud never felt that his work was finished. As new evidence came to him from his patients and his colleagues, he expanded and revised his basic theories. In the 1920's, for example, when Freud was seventy years old, he completely altered a number of his fundamental views. He revamped his theory of motivation, completely reversed his theory of anxiety, and instituted a new model of personality based upon the id, the ego, and the superego. One does not expect to find such flexibility in a man of seventy. Resistance to change is more characteristic of older people. But Freud cannot be judged by ordinary standards. He learned the lesson early in life that scientific conformity means intellectual stultification.

III. WHAT WAS FREUD?

What was Freud? By profession he was a physician. He treated sick people by methods that he himself had devised. Today he would be called a psychiatrist. Psychiatry is a branch of medicine that treats mental diseases and abnormalities. Freud was one of the founders of modern psychiatry.

Although he had to earn his living by practicing medicine, Freud was not by choice a medical doctor. In 1927 he confessed that "after forty-one years of medical activity, my self-knowledge tells me that I have never really been a doctor in the proper sense. I became a doctor through being compelled to deviate from my original purpose."

What was this original purpose? It was to understand some of the riddles of nature and to contribute something to their solution.

The most hopeful means of achieving this end seemed to be to enroll myself in the medical faculty; but even then I experimented—unsuccessfully—with zoology and chemistry, till at last, under the influence of Brücke, which carried more weight with me than any other in my whole life, I settled down to physiology, though in those days it was too narrowly restricted to histology.

By preference Freud was a scientist. As a young medical student and later in his connections with various hospitals, he made studies of physiological phenomena. He learned how to collect data by careful observation, to correlate his findings and draw conclusions, and to check his inferences by further observation. Although Freud did not make any outstanding discovery as a physiologist, this early experience in the laboratory provided him with excellent discipline in scientific method. It taught him how to be a scientist.

In the 1890's, Freud discovered what kind of scientist he wanted to be. In a letter to a friend he wrote, "It is psychology which has been the goal beckoning me from afar." For the rest of his life, some forty years, Freud was a psychologist.

What is the relation of psychology to psychoanalysis? Freud himself answered this question in 1927: "Psychoanalysis falls under the head of psychology; not of medical psychology in the old sense, nor of the psychology of morbid processes, but simply of psychology. It is certainly not the whole of psychology, but its substructure and perhaps even its entire foundation." Freud is here speaking of psychoanalysis as a theory of personality. But there is another side to psychoanalysis as well. Psychonalysis is also a method of psychotherapy. It consists of techniques for treating emotionally disturbed people. For Freud, the therapeutic aspects of psychoanalysis were secondary to the scientific and theoretical aspects. He did not want to see the therapy swallow up the science. It might be wise, therefore, to distinguish as we have done in this primer between Freudian psychology as a theoretical system of psychology, and psychoanalysis as a method of psychotherapy.

Physician, psychiatrist, scientist, psychologist—Freud was all of these things. But he was also something more. He was a philosopher. We get a hint of this in a letter he wrote to a friend in 1896. "As a young man I longed for nothing else than philosophical knowledge, and I am now on the way to satisfy that longing by passing over from medicine to psychology."

It was not at all unusual for the scientists of the nineteenth century to be attracted to philosophy. In fact, for many of them, science was philosophy. Does not philosophy mean "love of knowledge"? And what better way is there to show one's love of knowledge than by being a scientist? This was the substance of what Goethe was saying to every German intellectual. Goethe was the most influential voice in nineteenth-century thought and the idol of Germany. Freud was not immune to Gothe's influence. In fact, he decided upon a career in science after hearing Goethe's inspirational essay on Nature read aloud at a popular lecture.

Freud's philosophical interests were not those of the professional or academic philosopher. His philosophy was social and humanitarian. It took the form of building a philosophy of life. The Germans have a special word for it. They call it a *Weltanschauung,* which means "world-view." Freud stood for a philosophy of life that is based on science rather than on metaphysics or religion. He felt that a philosophy of life worth having is one based upon a true knowledge of man's nature, knowledge that could only be gained by scientific inquiry and research.

Freud did not feel that psychoanalysis was called upon to develop a new Weltanschauung. It was only necessary to extend the scientific world-view to the study of man. Freud's own philosophy of life can be summed up in a phrase: "Knowledge through science."

Freud's intimate knowledge of human nature made him both pessimistic and critical. He did not have a very high opinion of the bulk of mankind. He felt that the irrational forces in man's nature are so strong that the rational forces have little chance of success against them. A small minority might be able to live a life of reason, but most men are more comfortable living with their delusions and superstitions than with the truth. Freud had seen too many patients fighting vigorously to preserve their delusions to place much faith in the drawing power of logic and reason. Men resist knowing the truth about themselves. This pessimistic viewpoint is developed most fully in his book *The Future of an Illusion* although it provides the underlying mood for many of his writings.

Freud was also a social critic. He believed that society, which has been fashioned by man, reflects to a great extent man's irrationality. As a consequence, each new generation is corrupted by being born into an irrational society. The influence of man on society and of society on man is a vicious circle from which only a few hardy souls can free themselves.

Freud felt that the situation might be ameliorated by the application of psychological principles in raising and educating children. This would mean, of course, that parents and teachers would have to undergo a psychological re-education before they could be effective agents of reason and truth. Freud did not minimize the immensity of this task, but he did not know any other way by which to create a better society and better people. Freud's social criticism is presented in his book *Civilization and Its Discontents*.

What then was Freud? Physician, psychiatrist, psychoanalyst, psychologist, philosopher, and critic—these were his several vocations. Yet, taken separately or together, they do not really convey Freud's importance to the world. Although the word "genius" is used indiscriminately to describe a number of people, there is no other single word that fits Freud as well as this word does. He *was* a genius. One may prefer to think of him, as I do, as one of the few men in history who possessed a universal mind. Like Shakespeare and Goethe and Leonardo da Vinci, whatever Freud touched he illuminated. He was a very wise man.

CHAPTER TWO

The Organization of Personality

The total personality as conceived by Freud consists of three major systems. These are called the *id,* the *ego,* and the *superego.* In the mentally healthy person these three systems form a unified and harmonious organization. By working together co-operatively they enable the individual to carry on efficient and satisfying transactions with his environment. The purpose of these transactions is the fulfillment of man's basic needs and desires. Conversely, when the three systems of personality are at odds with one another the person is said to be maladjusted. He is dissatisfied with himself and with the world, and his efficiency is reduced.

I. THE ID

The sole function of the id is to provide for the immediate discharge of quantities of excitation (energy or tension) that are released in the organism by internal or external stimulation. This function of the id fulfills the primordial or initial principle of life which Freud called the *pleasure principle.* The aim of the pleasure principle is to rid the person of tension, or, if this is impossible— as it usually is—to reduce the amount of tension to a low level and to keep it as constant as possible. Tension is experienced as pain or discomfort, while relief from tension is experienced as pleasure or satisfaction. The aim of the pleasure principle may be said, then, to consist of avoiding pain and finding pleasure.

The pleasure principle is a special case of the universal

tendency found in all living matter to maintain constancy in the face of internal and external disturbances.

In its earliest form the id is a *reflex* apparatus that discharges immediately by motor pathways any sensory excitations reaching it. Thus when a very bright light falls upon the retina of the eye the eyelid closes and light is prevented from reaching the retina. Consequently the excitations that were produced in the nervous system by the light quiet down and the organism returns to a quiescent state. The organism is equipped with many such reflexes, as they are called, which serve the purpose of automatically discharging any bodily energy that has been released by a trigger, the stimulus, acting upon a sense organ. The typical consequence of the motor discharge is the removal of the stimulus. Sneezing, for example, usually expels whatever may be irritating the sensitive lining of the nose, and watering of the eyes flushes out foreign particles. The stimulus may come from within the body as well as from the outside world. One example of an internal stimulus is the reflex opening of the valve in the bladder when the pressure on it reaches a certain intensity. The excitation (tension) produced by the pressure is terminated by the emptying of the contents of the bladder through the open valve.

If all of the tensions that occur in the organism could be discharged by reflex action, there would be no need for any psychological development beyond that of the primitive reflex apparatus. Such is not the case, however. Many tensions occur for which there is no appropriate reflex discharge. For instance, when hunger contractions appear in the stomach of the baby, these contractions do not automatically produce food. Instead they produce restlessness and crying. Unless the baby is fed, the contractions increase in intensity until they are abolished by fatigue. In time, of course, the baby would die from starvation.

The hungry baby is not equipped with the necessary reflexes by which to satisfy its hunger, and were it not for the intervention of an older person bringing food the baby would perish. When food in a suitable form is brought to the infant's mouth, sucking, swallowing, and digestive reflexes carry on unaided and bring the tension of hunger to an end.

There would be no psychological development if every time the baby began to feel the tension of hunger it was immediately fed and if all of the other excitations arising in the body were similarly discharged by the co-operative efforts of parental care and inborn reflexes. However, in spite of the solicitude of parents, they are not likely to anticipate and quickly satisfy all of the baby's needs. In fact, by the use of schedules and the institution of training and discipline, parents create tensions as well as reduce them. The baby inevitably experiences some degree of frustration and discomfort. These experiences stimulate the development of the id.

The new development that takes place in the id as a result of frustration is called the *primary process*. In order to understand the nature of the primary process it will be necessary to discuss some of the psychological potentialities of the human being. The psychological apparatus has a sensory end and a motor end. The sensory end consists of the sense organs, which are specialized structures for receiving stimuli, and the motor end consists of muscles, which are the organs of action and movement. For reflex action it is only necessary to possess sense organs and muscles and an intervening nervous system that transmits messages in the form of nervous impulses from the sensory end to the motor end.

In addition to a sensory system and a motor system, the individual has a perceptual system and a memory system. The perceptual system receives excitations from the sense organs and forms a mental picture or representation of the object that is being presented to the sense organs. These mental pictures are preserved as memory traces in the memory system. When the memory traces are activated, the person is said to have a memory image of the object that he originally perceived. The past is brought into the present by means of these memory images. The perception is a mental representation of an object, while the memory image is a mental representation of a perception. When we look at something in the world, a perception is formed; when we remember what we once saw a memory image is formed.

Now let us return to the case of the hungry baby. In the past whenever the baby was hungry it was eventually fed. During the feeding, the baby sees, tastes, smells, and feels the food, and these perceptions are stored in its memory system. Through repetition, food becomes associated with tension-reduction. Then if the baby is not fed immediately the tension of hunger produces a memory image of food, with which it is associated. Thus there exists in the id an image of the object which is capable of reducing the tension of hunger. The process which produces a memory image of an object that is needed to reduce a tension is called the *primary process*.

The primary process attempts to discharge tension by establishing what Freud called "an identity of perception." By an identity of perception Freud meant that the id considers the memory image to be identical with the perception itself. For the id, the memory of food is exactly the same as having the food itself. In other words, the id fails to distinguish between a *subjective* memory image and an *objective* perception of the real object. A familiar illustration of the action of the primary process is the thirsty traveler who imagines he sees water. Another example of the primary process is the nocturnal dream. A dream is a succession of images, usually visual in quality, whose function it is to reduce tension by reviving memories of past events and objects that are associated in some way with gratification. The hungry sleeper dreams of food and things associated with eating, while the sexually aroused sleeper dreams of sexual activities and related events. The formation of an image of a tension-reducing object is called *wish-fulfillment*. Freud believed that all dreams are wish-fulfillments or attempted wish-fulfillments. We dream about what we want.

Obviously a hungry person cannot make a meal of food images nor can a thirsty person slake his thirst by drinking imaginary water. In the case of the dreamer, Freud thought that dreaming of desirable objects and events might serve the purpose of preventing the sleeper from awakening. Even in waking life the primary process is not entirely useless, since it is necessary to know—i.e., have an image of—what one needs before one can set about getting it. A hungry person who has a mental representation of food is in a better position to satisfy his hunger than is a person who does not know what to look for. Were it not for the primary process, a person could satisfy his needs only through aimless trial-and-error behavior. Because the primary process by itself does not reduce tensions effectively, a *secondary process* is developed. But the secondary process belongs to the ego, so we will defer a discussion of it to the next section.

Freud had other things to say about the id. The id is the primary source of psychic energy and the seat of the instincts. (For a discussion of energy and instincts, see Chapter 3, "The Dynamics of Personality.") The id is in closer touch with the body and its processes than with the external world. The id lacks organization as compared with the ego and the superego. Its energy is in a mobile state so that it can be readily discharged or displaced from one object to another. The id does not change with the passage of time; it cannot be modified by experience because it is not in contact with the external world. However, it can be controlled and regulated by the ego.

The id is not governed by laws of reason or logic, and it does not possess values, ethics, or morality. It is driven by one consideration only, to obtain satisfaction for instinctual needs in accordance with the pleasure principle. There are only two possible issues for any id process. Either it discharges in action or wish-fulfillment, or it succumbs to the influence of the ego, in which case the energy becomes *bound* instead of being immediately discharged.

Freud speaks of the id as being the true psychic reality. By this he means that the id is the primary subjective reality, the inner world that exists before the individual has had experience of the external world. Not only are the instincts and reflexes inborn, but the images that are produced by tension states may also be innate. This means that a hungry baby can have an image of food without having to learn to associate food with hunger. Freud believed that experiences that are repeated with great frequency and intensity in many individuals of successive generations become permanent deposits in the id. New deposits are made in the id during the life of a person as a result of the mechanism of *repression*. (Repression is discussed in Chapter 4, "The Development of Personality.")

Not only is the id archaic from the standpoint of racial history, but it is also archaic in the life of the individual. It is the foundation upon which the personality is built. The id retains its infantile character throughout life. It cannot tolerate tension. It wants immediate gratification. It is demanding, impulsive, irrational, asocial, selfish, and pleasure-loving. It is the spoiled child of the personality. It is omnipotent because it has the magical power of fulfilling its wishes by imagination, fantasy, hallucinations, and dreams. It is said to be oceanic because, like the sea, it contains everything. It recognizes nothing external to itself. The id is the world of subjective reality in which the pursuit of pleasure and the avoidance of pain are the only functions that count.

Freud acknowledges that the id is the obscure and inaccessible part of personality, and that what little is known about it has been learned from the study of dreams and neurotic symptoms. However, we can see the id in action whenever a person does something impulsive. A person, for example, who acts on an impulse to throw a rock through a window or trip someone up or commit rape is under the domination of the id. Similarly, a person who spends a lot of time daydreaming and building castles in the air is being controlled by his id. The id does not think. It only wishes or acts.

II. THE EGO

The two processes by which the id discharges tension, namely, impulsive motor activity and image formation (wish-fulfillment), do not suffice to attain the great evolutionary goals of survival and reproduction. Neither reflexes nor wishes will provide the hungry person with food nor the sexually motivated person with a mate. In fact, impulsive behavior may result in an increase of tension (pain) by calling forth punishment from the external world. Unless he has a permanent caretaker, as he has during infancy, man must seek and find food, a sex partner, and many other goal objects necessary for life. In order to accomplish these missions successfully it is necessary for him to take into account external reality (the environment) and, either by accommodating himself to it or by asserting mastery over it, obtain from the world that which he needs. These transactions between the person and the world require the formation of a new psychological system, the *ego*.

In the well-adjusted person the ego is the executive of the personality, controlling and governing the id and the superego and maintaining commerce with the external world in the interest of the total personality and its far-flung needs. When the ego is performing its executive functions wisely, harmony and adjustment prevail. Should the ego abdicate or surrender too much of its power to the id, to the superego, or to the external world, disharmony and maladjustments will ensue.

Instead of the pleasure principle the ego is governed by the *reality principle*. Reality means that which exists. The aim of the reality principle is to postpone the discharge of energy until the actual object that will satisfy the need has been discovered or produced. For example, the child has to learn not to put just anything into his mouth when he is hungry. He has to learn to recognize food, and to put off eating until he has located an edible object. Otherwise, he will have some painful experiences.

The postponement of action means that the ego has to be able to tolerate tension until the tension can be discharged by an appropriate form of behavior. The institution of the reality principle does not mean that the pleasure principle is forsaken. It is only temporarily suspended in the interest of reality. Eventually, the reality principle leads to pleasure, although a person may have to endure some discomfort while he is looking for reality.

The reality principle is served by a process which Freud called the *secondary process* because it is developed after and overlays the primary process of the id. In order to understand what is meant by the secondary process it is necessary to see just where the primary process gets the individual in the satisfaction of his needs. It gets him only to the point where he has a picture of the object that will satisfy the need. The next step is to find or produce the object, that is, to bring it into existence. This step is accomplished by means of the secondary process. The secondary process consists of discovering or producing reality by means of a plan of action that has been developed through thought and reason (cognition). The secondary process is nothing more or less than what is ordinarily called problem solving or thinking.

When a person puts a plan of action into effect in order to see whether it will work or not, he is said to be engaging in *reality testing*. If the test does not work, that is, if the desired object is not discovered or produced, a new plan of action is thought out and tested. This continues until the correct solution (reality) is found and the tension is discharged by a suitable action. In the case of hunger, the suitable action would consist of eating food.

The secondary process accomplishes what the primary process is unable to do, namely, to separate the subjective world of the mind from the objective world of physical reality. The secondary process does not make the mistake, as the primary process does, of regarding the image of an object as though it were the object itself.

The inauguration of the reality principle, the functioning of the secondary process, and the more significant role that the external world comes to play in the life of a person, stimulate the growth and elaboration of the psychological processes of perception, memory, thinking, and action.

The perceptual system develops finer powers of discrimination so that the external world is perceived with greater accuracy and precision. It learns to scan the world rapidly and to select from the welter of stimuli only those features of the environment that are relevant to the problem to be solved. In addition to the information that is obtained through the sense organs, thinking makes use of information that has been stored in the memory system. Memory is improved by the formation of associations between memory traces, and by the development of a system of notation: language. One's judgment becomes sharper, so that it is easier to make clear-cut decisions as to whether something is true (actually exists) or whether it is false (does not exist). Another important series of changes takes place in the motoric system. The person learns to handle his muscles more skillfully and to carry on more complex patterns of movement. All in all, these adaptations in psychological functions enable the person to behave more intelligently and more efficiently and to master his impulses and his environment in the interest of greater satisfaction and pleasure. The ego may be thought of as a complex organization of psychological processes that acts as an intermediary between the id and the external world.

In addition to the processes that serve reality, there is an ego function that resembles the primary process of the id. This is a function that produces phantasies and daydreams. It is free from the demands of reality testing and is subordinate to the pleasure principle. However, this ego process differs from the primary process because it distinguishes between phantasy and reality, which is not the case with the primary process. Phantasies produced by the ego are recognized for what they are, namely, playful and pleasurable imaginings. Although they are never mistaken for reality, they provide a holiday from the more serious business of the ego.

Although the ego is largely a product of an interaction with the environment, its lines of development are laid down by heredity and guided by natural growth processes (maturation). This means that every person has inborn potentialities for thinking and reasoning. The realization of these potentialities is brought about by experience, training, and education. All formal education, for example, has as its main objective teaching people how to think more effectively. Effective thinking consists of being able to arrive at the truth, truth being defined as that which exists.

III. THE SUPEREGO

The third major institution of personality, the *super-ego*, is the moral or judicial branch of personality. It represents the ideal rather than the real, and it strives for perfection rather than for reality or pleasure. The superego is the person's moral code. It develops out of the ego as a consequence of the child's assimilation of his parents' standards regarding what is good and virtuous and what is bad and sinful. By assimilating the moral authority of his parents, the child replaces their authority with his own inner authority. The internalization of parental authority enables the child to control his behavior in line with their wishes, and by doing so to secure their approval and avoid their displeasure. In other words, the child learns that he not only has to obey the reality principle in order to obtain pleasure and avoid pain, but that he also has to try to behave according to the moral dictates of his parents. The relatively long period during which the child is dependent upon the parents favors the formation of the superego.

The superego is made up of two subsystems, the *ego-ideal* and the *conscience*. The ego-ideal corresponds to the child's conceptions of what his parents consider to be morally good. The parents convey their standards of virtue to the child by rewarding him for conduct which is in line with these standards. For example, if he is consistently rewarded for being neat and tidy then neatness is apt to become one of his ideals. Conscience, on the other hand, corresponds to the child's conceptions of what his parents feel is morally bad, and these are established through experiences with punishment. If he has been frequently punished for getting dirty, then dirtiness is considered to be something bad. Ego-ideal and conscience are opposite sides of the same moral coin.

What are the rewards and punishments by which parents control the formation of the child's superego? They are of two kinds, physical and psychological. Physical rewards consist of objects that are desired by the child. They are such things as food, toys, mother, father, caresses, and sweets. Physical punishments are painful assaults upon the body of the child such as spankings and deprivation of things he wants. The principal psychological reward is that of parental approval expressed either by word or facial expression. Approval stands for love. By the same token, withdrawal of love is the main form of psychological punishment. This is expressed by verbal admonitions or disapproving looks. Of course, physical rewards and punishments may also mean love or withdrawal of love to the child. The child who has received a spanking not only hurts but he also may feel that the punishing parent has rejected him, i.e., withdrawn love. However the bestowal or withdrawal of affection derives its power over the child in the first place by virtue of its connection with the satisfaction or dissatisfaction of basic needs. A child desires his mother's love because he has learned that an unloving mother is likely to withhold food and thereby prolong a painful state of tension. Similarly, a child tries to avoid incurring the disapproval of his father because he has learned that a disapproving father may create a painful state by spanking him. In the final analysis, rewards and punishments, whatever their sources may be, are conditions that reduce or increase inner tension.

In order for the superego to have the same control over the child that the parents have, it is necessary for the superego to have the power to enforce its moral rules. Like the parents, the superego enforces its rules by rewards and punishments. These rewards and punishments are conferred upon the ego because the ego, by virtue of its control over the actions of the person, is held responsible for the occurrence of moral and immoral acts. If the action is in accordance with the ethical standards of the superego, the ego is rewarded. However, it is not necessary for the ego to permit an actual physical action to take place in order for it to be rewarded or punished by the superego. The ego may be rewarded or punished for merely *thinking* of doing something. A thought is the same as a deed in the eyes of the superego. In this respect the superego resembles the id, which also makes no distinction between subjective and objective. This explains why a person who lives a very virtuous life may nevertheless suffer many pangs of conscience. The superego punishes the ego for thinking bad thoughts even though the thoughts may never be translated into action.

What rewards and punishments are available to the superego? They may be either physical or psychological. The superego may say, in effect, to the person who has followed the path of virtue, "Now that you have been good for a long time, you will be allowed to indulge yourself and have a good time." It may be an expensive meal, a long rest, or sexual gratification. A vacation, for example, is usually regarded as a reward for hard work.

To the moral transgressor the superego may say, in effect, "Now that you have been bad, you will be punished by having something unpleasant happen to you." The misfortune may be an upset stomach, an injury, or the loss of a valuable possession. It is this insight of Freud's into the intricate and subtle workings of the human personality that revealed an important reason why people get sick, have accidents, and lose things. All misfortunes may involve, to a greater or a lesser extent, self-punishment for having done something wrong. An example of this is the young man who wrecked his car shortly after he had had sexual relations with a girl. Of course, a person is usually not aware of the connection between having a guilty conscience and having an accident.

The psychological rewards and punishments employed by the superego are feelings of pride and feelings of guilt or inferiority, respectively. The ego becomes flushed with pride when it has behaved virtuously or thought virtuous thoughts, and it feels ashamed of itself when it has yielded to temptation. Pride is equivalent to self-love, and guilt or inferiority to self-hate; they are the inner representations of parental love and parental rejection.

The superego is the representative in the personality of the traditional values and ideals of society as they are handed down from parents to children. In this connection it should be borne in mind that the child's superego is not a reflection of the parents' conduct but rather of the parents' superegos. An adult may say one thing and do another, but it is what he says, backed up by threats or gifts, that counts in the shaping of the child's ethical standards. In addition to the parents, other agents of society take a hand in the formation of the child's superego. Teachers, ministers, policemen—in fact anyone who is in a position of authority over the child—may function in the role of parents. The child's reactions to these figures of authority are largely determined, however, by what he has assimilated earlier from his parents.

What purpose does the superego serve? Primarily it serves the purpose of controlling and regulating those impulses whose uncontrolled expression would endanger the stability of society. These impulses are sex and aggression. The disobedient, rebellious, or sexually curious child is regarded as being bad and immoral. The adult who is sexually promiscuous or who breaks laws and is generally destructive and antisocial is considered to be a wicked person. The superego, by placing inner restraints upon lawlessness and anarchy. enables a person to become a law-abiding member of society.

If the id is regarded as the product of evolution and the psychological representative of one's biological endowment, and the ego is the resultant of one's interaction with objective reality and the province of the higher mental processes, then the superego may be said to be the product of socialization and the vehicle of cultural tradition.

The reader should bear in mind that there are no sharp boundaries between the three systems. Just because they have different names does not mean that they are separate entities. The names, id, ego and superego, actually signify nothing in themselves. They are merely a shorthand way of designating different processes, functions, mechanisms, and dynamisms within the total personality.

The ego is formed out of the id and the superego is formed out of the ego. They continue to interact and blend with each other throughout life. These interactions and blendings, as well as the oppositions that develop among the three systems, constitute the subject matter of the next chapter.

REFERENCES

FREUD, SIGMUND. (1900.) *The Interpretation of Dreams,* Chap. 7. London: The Hogarth Press, 1953.

FREUD, SIGMUND. (1911.) "Formulations Regarding the Two Principles in Mental Functioning." In *Collected Papers,* Vol. IV, pp. 13-21. London: The Hogarth Press, 1946.

FREUD, SIGMUND. (1923.) *The Ego and the Id.* London: The Hogarth Press, 1947.

FREUD, SIGMUND. (1925.) "A Note upon the 'Mystic Writing Pad.'" In *Collected Papers,* Vol. V, pp. 175-80. London: The Hogarth Press, 1950.

FREUD, SIGMUND. (1925.) "Negation." In *Collected Papers,* Vol. V, pp. 181-85. London: The Hogarth Press, 1950.

FREUD, SIGMUND. (1933.) *New Introductory Lectures on Psychoanalysis,* Chap. 3. New York: W. W. Norton & Company, Inc., 1933.

FREUD, SIGMUND. (1938.) *An Outline of Psychoanalysis,* Chap. I. New York: W. W. Norton & Company, Inc., 1949.

CHAPTER THREE

The Dynamics of Personality

In the previous chapter we took up the organization of personality and described some of the prominent processes and functions of its three provinces, the id, the ego, and the superego. In this chapter our purpose is to show how these three systems operate and how they interact with one another and with the environment.

I. PSYCHIC ENERGY

The human organism is a complicated energy system, deriving its energy from the food it eats and expending it for such purposes as circulation, respiration, digestion, nervous conduction, muscular activity, perceiving, remembering, and thinking. There is no reason to believe that the energy which runs the organism is essentially any different from the energy which runs the universe. Energy takes many forms—mechanical, thermal, electrical, and chemical—and is capable of being transformed from one form into another. The form of energy which operates the three systems of personality is called *psychic energy*. There is nothing mystical, vitalistic, or supernatural about the concept of psychic energy. It performs work or is capable of performing work as does any form of energy. Psychic energy performs psychological work —e.g., thinking, perceiving, and remembering—just as mechanical energy performs mechanical work.

One can speak of the transformation of bodily energy into psychic energy as well as the transformation of psychic energy into bodily energy. These transformations are continually taking place. We think (psychic energy) and then we act (muscular energy), or we are stimulated by a pattern of sound waves (mechanical energy) and we hear (psychic energy) someone talking. Just how these transformations take place is not known.

II. INSTINCT

All of the energy used for performing the work of the personality is obtained from the *instincts*. An instinct is defined as an inborn condition which imparts direction to psychological processes. The sex instinct, for example, directs the psychological processes of perceiving, remembering, and thinking toward the goal of sexual consummation. An instinct is like a river that flows along a particular waterway.

An instinct has a *source*, an *aim*, an *object*, and an *impetus*. The principal sources of instinctual energy are bodily needs or impulses. A need or impulse is an excitatory process in some tissue or organ of the body which releases energy that is stored in the body. For example, the physical condition of hunger activates the hunger instinct by providing it with energy. This instinctual energy then imparts goal-direction to the psychological processes of perception, memory, and thought. One looks for food, tries to remember where food has been found on previous occasions, or plans a course of action by which food can be obtained.

The final aim of an instinct is the removal of a bodily need. The aim of the instinct of hunger, for example, is to remove the physical condition of hunger. When this is done, no more bodily energy is released, the hunger instinct disappears, and the individual returns to a state of physiological and psychological quiescence. Stated in another way, the aim of an instinct is to eliminate the source of that instinct.

In addition to the final aim of quiescence, Freud observed that there are also subordinate aims that have to be fulfilled before the final aim can be reached. Before hunger can be appeased it is necessary to find food and take it into one's mouth. The finding and eating of food are subordinate to the elimination of hunger. Freud called the final goal of an instinct its *internal aim*, and the subordinate goals of an instinct its *external aims*.

An instinct is said to be *conservative* because its goal is to return a person to the quiescent state which existed prior to disturbance by an excitatory process. The course of an instinct is always from a state of tension to a state of relaxation. In some instances, notably in the satisfaction of the sex impulse, there is a mounting of tension prior to the final discharge. This in no way refutes the general principle of instinct functioning, because the ultimate aim of the sex drive is relief from excitation no matter how much tension may be generated prior to the final discharge. In fact, people learn to build up a lot of tension because the sudden release of large quantities of tension is very pleasurable.

In other words, an instinct always tries to bring about a *regression* to an earlier condition. This tendency of an instinct to repeat over and over again the cycle from excitation to repose is called the *repetition compulsion*. There are numerous examples of repetition compulsion in everyday life. The periodic and regular phases of waking activity followed by sleep is one example. Three meals a day is another. Sexual desire followed by sexual gratification is still another.

In summary, then, the aim of an instinct is characterized by being conservative, regressive, and repetitive.

The object of an instinct is the object or means by which the aim is accomplished. The object of the hunger instinct is eating food; of the sex instinct, copulation; and of the aggressive instinct, fighting. The object or means is the most variable feature of an instinct, since many different objects and activities can take the place of one another. As we shall see in Chapter 4 on the development of personality, the elaboration of the means by which instincts reach their goal of tension-reduction constitutes one of the principal avenues of personality development.

The impetus of an instinct is its strength or force,

which is determined by the amount of energy that it possesses. Strong hunger exerts a greater impulsion upon the psychological processes than weak hunger does. When a person is very hungry, his mind dwells upon food to the exclusion of practically everything else. Similarly, when a person is very much in love, it is hard for him to think about anything else.

The seat of the instincts is the id. Since the instincts constitute the total amount of psychic energy, the id is said to be the original reservoir of psychic energy. In order to form the ego and superego, energy is withdrawn from this pool. How this withdrawal takes place is the subject of the next section.

III. THE DISTRIBUTION AND DISPOSAL OF PSYCHIC ENERGY

A. THE ID   The energy of the id is used for instinctual gratification by means of reflex action and wish-fulfillment. In reflex action as exemplified by the eating of food, the emptying of the bladder, and the sexual orgasm, energy is automatically discharged in motor action. In wish-fulfillment, energy is used to produce an image of the instinctual object. The aim of both processes is to expend the instinctual energy in ways that will eliminate the need and bring repose to the individual.

The investment of energy in the image of an object, or the expenditure of energy in discharge action upon an object that will satisfy an instinct, is called *object-choice* or *object-cathexis*. All of the energy of the id is expended in object-cathexes.

The energy invested by the id in object-choices is very fluid. This means the energy can be shunted easily from one object to another. This shunting of energy is called *displacement*. Thus, if food is not handy, a hungry baby may place a wooden block or its own hand in its mouth. For the baby, before he has learned to discriminate, food, a wooden block, or its hand are all the same. Objects are regarded as being equivalent when there are specific and concrete resemblances between them. Two objects such as a bottle of milk and a block, for example, are perceived as being identical because they can both be taken hold of by the hand and brought to the mouth. The energy of the id is very displaceable because the id is not capable of making fine distinctions between objects.

The tendency of the id to treat objects as though they were the same, in spite of differences between them, produces a distorted form of thinking which is called *predicate thinking*. When two objects, for instance a tree and the male sex organ, are equated in a person's mind because they both share the same physical characteristic of protruding, that person is doing predicate thinking. This type of thinking is particularly prevalent in dreams, and accounts for dream symbolism. Riding horseback or plowing a field may stand for or symbolize sexual intercourse because similar movements are performed in riding, plowing, and copulating. Predicate thinking is common in waking life too, causing a great deal of confusion in a person's thinking by preventing him from making proper discriminations. Race prejudice is often due to predicate thinking. Because Negroes are dark-skinned and because darkness is associated with wickedness and dirt, Negroes are thought of as being bad and dirty. Likewise, red-haired people are thought to have fiery tempers because red is a fiery color.

When the directional flow of instinctual energy is blocked by ego or superego processes, it tries to break through the resistances and discharge itself in phantasy or action. When the breakthrough is successful, the rational processes of the ego are undermined. The person makes mistakes in speaking, writing, talking, perceiving, and remembering, and he has accidents because he becomes confused and loses contact with reality. His ability to solve problems and to discover reality is diminished by the intrusion of impulsive wishes. Everyone knows how hard it is to keep one's mind on one's work when one is hungry or sexually excited or angry. When the id is not successful in finding direct outlets for instinctual energy, the energy is taken over by the ego or the superego and used to energize the operations of these systems.

B. THE EGO   The ego has no energy of its own. Indeed it cannot be said to exist until energy has been diverted from the id into the latent processes that constitute the ego. With the energizing of these new processes —such as discrimination, memory, judgment, and reasoning—which have existed up to this time as innate and latent tendencies in the personality, the ego as a separate system begins its lengthy and complex development.

The point of departure for the activation of these latent ego potentialities lies in a mechanism known as *identification*. In order to understand the nature of this mechanism it will be necessary to go back over some of the ground we have already covered. It will be recalled that the id makes no distinction between subjective imagery and objective reality. When it cathects an image of an object, that is, when energy is invested in a process which forms a mental representation of an object, it is the same as cathecting the object itself. For the id, object as image and object as external reality are identities and not separate entities.

The failure of the id to obtain relief from tension brings about the emergence of a new line of development which lays a foundation for the formation of the ego. Instead of an image and the real object being regarded as identities, a separation between the two takes place. What happens as a result of this differentiation is that the purely subjective, internal world of the id becomes divided into a subjective, inner world (the mind) and an objective, outer world (the environment). If he is to be properly adjusted, the person is now confronted with the task of bringing these two worlds into harmony with one another. Mental states have to be synchronized with reality if the person is to be properly adjusted.

For example, when a hungry person has a memory image of food, he has to locate a real object in the environment that matches his memory image. If the memory image is an accurate one, the object he will find will be food. If the memory image is not an accurate representation of food, it will have to be revised until it is. Otherwise, the hungry person will starve to death. At one time, the earth was believed to be flat, but this conception was revised when Columbus and other explorers showed that the world was round and not flat. All advances in knowledge consist of making one's mental representations of the world more accurate pictures of the world as it really is.

The work of making the contents of the mind faithful and accurate replicas of the contents of the external world is performed by the secondary process. When the idea of an object agrees with the object itself, the idea is said to be identified with the object. The identification of thoughts with reality must be close and exact in order that the thought-out plan of action should actually bring the person to his goal.

As a result of this mechanism of identification, energy which was invested by the id in images without regard for, and indeed with no conception of, reality is diverted into the formation of accurate mental representations of the real world. At this point, logical thinking takes the place of wish-fulfillment. This diversion of energy from the id into cognitive processes marks the initial step in the development of the ego.

It is important to bear in mind that this new adaptation of the personality is contingent upon the separation of subject (mind) and object (matter). For the id there is no such separation. Consequently, no identification is possible. The identity of image and object in the id might be regarded as a kind of primitive identification. It is better, however, to use the term *identity* for this condition and to reserve the term *identification* for those cases where there is a clear recognition of a separation of the two things that are being identified, namely, mental events and external reality.

The separation between mind and the physical world of reality takes place as a result of frustration and learning. As we have said before, the id cannot satisfy the vital needs of life by reflex action or wish-fulfillment alone. Consequently, the person just has to learn the difference between images and reality if he is going to survive. Undoubtedly, there is an inborn predisposition to discriminate between inner mental states and outer reality, but this predisposition has to be developed by experience and training. From a very early age, the baby is learning to differentiate between what is outside in the world and what is inside in the mind. Moreover, through experience and education, he learns to make what is in his mind agree with what actually exists outside his mind. He learns, in other words, to identify the two.

An example of the difference between identity and identification might make the meaning of the two terms clearer. When a person dreams that he is being chased by a lion, he ordinarily feels as though a real lion were chasing him. During a dream, the images are not distinguished from the real objects that they represent. They are identities. Consequently, a dreamer experiences the same emotion he would feel if the events of the dream were actually taking place. Similarly, a person who has a hallucination does not distinguish it from reality. On the other hand, if a person in waking life is watching television or reading a book, he does not think that the pictures or the words are the actual objects themselves. He realizes that they are only representations of reality. He may identify the events in the television program or in the book with reality, but he is rarely deluded into thinking that they are reality itself.

By identification with the objects of the external world, the subjective representations of these objects receive the cathexes that were formerly invested by the id in the objects themselves. These new cathexes are called *ego-cathexes* to distinguish them from the instinctual object-choices of the id. By means of identification, then, energy is made available for the development of realistic thinking (the secondary process), which takes the place of hallucinatory wish-fulfillment (the primary process). This redistribution of energy from the id to the ego is a major dynamical event in the development of personality.

Because the rational functions of the ego are so successful in obtaining gratification for the instincts, more and more of the energy from the reservoir in the id is siphoned off into the ego. As the ego waxes in strength the id wanes. However, should the ego fail in its task of satisfying the demands of the id, ego-cathexes are reconverted into instinctual object-cathexes and infantile wish-fulfillment reigns again. This is what happens during sleep. Because the ego cannot function efficiently during sleep, the primary process is invoked and produces hallucinatory images. Even during waking life, the primary process may be reactivated when the ego does not produce results directly. This is known as *autistic* or *wishful thinking*.

A person who wants very much for something to be true often fools himself into thinking it is true. We all know how easy it is to let our biases and desires direct our thinking. Even the objective scientist has to be careful not to let his theoretical preferences influence his observations and reasoning. That is why he is careful to provide suitable controls for his experiments and observations, and to repeat them again and again to make sure that what he saw the first time was really true. Wishful thinking is continually setting traps for us.

Under normal conditions the ego pretty much monopolizes the store of psychic energy. When it has attracted sufficient energy away from the id, it can use this energy for other purposes than that of satisfying the instincts. Energy is used to develop the psychological processes of perceiving, attending, learning, remembering, judging, discriminating, reasoning, and imagining. All of these processes become greatly elaborated and more efficient as the ego gains control of the energy. The world takes on new meanings for a person as he learns more and more about it, and with his increased knowledge he is in a better position to bend the world to his own purposes. Not only in the development of the individual but also in the racial and cultural evolution of man there is an ever-increasing control over nature by the diversion of energy from the non-rational processes of the id into the rational ones of the ego.

Some of the energy of the ego has to be used to inhibit and postpone the outflow of excitations through the motor system. The purpose of this postponement is to permit the ego to work out a realistic plan of action before it acts. When energy is used to block the flow of energy in the direction of final discharge, these blocking forces are called *anti-cathexes*. An anti-cathexis is a charge of energy that opposes a cathexis. The anti-cathexes of the ego are directed against the id-cathexes because these cathexes press for immediate relief from tension. The boundary region between the ego and the id might be likened to the boundary between two countries, one of which is trying to invade the other. The country which is threatened with invasion erects fortifications (anti-cathexes of the ego) by which to repulse the invader (id-cathexes). When the anti-cathexes fail to hold, the object-cathexes of the id overwhelm the ego and produce impulsive behavior. This is what happens when an ordinarily controlled person loses his temper.

The energy in the ego may also be used to form new object-cathexes. These objects do not directly satisfy the basic needs of the organism, although they are connected by associative links with objects that do. For example, the hunger instinct may branch out in many directions and encompass many activities that are not essential to the satisfaction of hunger. Collecting unusual recipes and cookbooks, acquiring fine china and silverware, installing a model electric kitchen, discovering restaurants that serve exotic foods, reading and talking about food and numerous other food-oriented and food-associated interests engage the energies of many people, although none of these interests by itself actually reduces hunger.

The reason the ego has enough energy to devote to non-instinctual purposes is that its efficient functioning yields a surplus of energy over and above that needed for the vital necessities of life. The greater the economy with which the ego operates in gratifying bodily needs, the more energy it has for leisure-time activities. The way in which these ego interests, as they are called, originate is discussed in the next chapter.

Finally, the energy of the ego is used to effect a synthesis or integration of the three systems of personality. The purpose of this synthesis is to produce inner harmony and smooth transactions with the environment. When the ego is performing its synthetic function wisely, the id, ego, and superego are blended together into a unified, well-organized whole. We shall have more to say about the synthetic function of the ego in succeeding chapters.

By comparison with the mobility of the energy in the id, the energy of the ego is a good deal less fluid and a great deal more bound. By the binding of energy is meant that it is invested in mental operations and not expended in impulsive action or wish-fulfillment. The ego binds energy by channeling it into psychological processes, by investing it in anti-cathexes, by forming ego interests, and by using it for synthesis. As the ego develops, it commits more and more of its energy to these functions.

C. THE SUPEREGO   Fear of punishment and desire for approval cause the child to identify himself with the moral precepts of his parents. This identification with the parents results in the formation of the superego. Unlike the realistic identifications of the ego, however, the identifications upon which the superego is based are those of idealized and omnipotent parents. The parents are invested with great powers of punishing and rewarding the child. Consequently, the superego is also furnished with the power to reward and to punish. The former is done by the ego-ideal, the latter by the conscience.

The prohibitions of the conscience are inhibitions or anti-cathexes which block the discharge of instinctual energy either directly in impulsive behavior and wish-fulfillment, or indirectly by way of ego mechanisms. That is, the conscience opposes both the id and the ego, and tries to suspend the operation of the pleasure principle and the reality principle. A person who has a strong conscience is constantly on guard against immoral impulses. He spends so much of his energy for defense against the id that he does not have enough to perform useful and satisfying work. As a consequence, he becomes immobilized and lives a strait-jacket existence.

The anti-cathexes of the conscience differ from those of the ego. The resisting forces of the ego serve the purpose of delaying final action in order that the ego can work out a satisfactory plan. The prohibitions of conscience, on the other hand, attempt to abolish all thought of action whatsoever. The conscience says "No" to the instincts, while the ego says "Wait."

The ego-ideal strives for perfection. Its energy is invested in cathecting ideals which are the internalized representatives of the parents' moral values. These ideals represent perfectionistic object-choices. A person who has a lot of his energy tied up in the ego-ideal is idealistic and high-minded. His choice of objects and interests is determined more by their moralistic than by their realistic values. He is more concerned with differentiating the good from the bad than he is with distinguishing between the true and the false. For such a person, virtue is more important than truth.

By identifying with the ethical object-choices of the ego-ideal, the ego experiences feelings of pride. Pride is the reward that the ego-ideal confers upon the ego for being good. It is analogous to the feeling that the child has when he is praised by his parents. On the other hand, when the ego identifies with or chooses an object that is considered unworthy by the superego, the superego punishes the ego by making it feel ashamed and guilty. This, too, closely resembles the situation that occurs when a child is punished by his mother or father for being naughty.

Pride is a form of *secondary narcissism*. The ego loves itself for doing what is virtuous. "Virtue is its own reward." By the same token it might be said that sin is its own punishment.

Thus we see that the energy from the id becomes channeled into the ego and the superego by the mechanism of identification. The energy may then be used by the ego and superego to forward or to frustrate the aim of the id, which is to seek pleasure (freedom from tension) and to avoid pain (increase of tension). We have seen how the ego allies itself with the id for the purpose of gratifying the instincts. It would seem, on the other hand, that the superego, as the foe of the immoral, pleasure-loving instincts, should always oppose the id. But this is not always the case. The superego can be manipulated by the id for the purpose of gaining satisfaction for the instincts. That is, the superego can act as the agent of the id both in relation to the external world and to the ego. For example, the superego of a moralistic person can become very aggressive against his ego. The ego is made to feel unworthy and wicked. A person who feels this way may even do himself bodily harm or commit suicide. Acts of self-aggression satisfy the aggressive impulses of the id.

The superego of a very high-minded person can also gain satisfaction for the id by attacking people who are considered to be immoral. Cruelty masquerading as moral indignation is not unknown and has even been practiced on a large scale. Witness, for example, the brutality of the Inquisition, the burning of witches, and the mass murders perpetrated by the Nazis. Ostensibly, these sadistic attacks were instigated by moral fervor of the highest order. Actually, however, they represent the expression of primitive id forces. In such cases, the superego is said to be corrupted by the id.

The id and the superego have another quality in common. They both function irrationally and distort and falsify reality. Rather, we should say, the id and the superego distort the realistic thinking of the ego. The superego forces the ego to see things as they should be and not as they are. The id forces the ego to see the world as the id wishes it would be. In either case, the secondary process, reality testing, and the reality principle are perverted by irrational forces.

In conclusion of this section on the distribution and disposal of psychic energy in the personality, it should be borne in mind that there is only so much available energy and no more. This means that if the ego gains energy, the id or the superego—or both—have to lose energy. The energizing of one system of personality means the de-energizing of other systems. A person with a strong ego will have a weak id and superego.

The dynamics of personality consists of the changes in the distribution of energy throughout the personality. The conduct of a person is determined by his dynamics. If the bulk of the energy is controlled by the superego, his conduct will be moralistic. If it is controlled by the ego his behavior will be realistic. And if it is retained by the id, which is the source of all psychic energy, his actions will be impulsive. What a person is and does is inevitably an expression of the way in which the energy is distributed.

IV. CATHEXIS AND ANTI-CATHEXIS

In one of his writings Freud characterizes psychoanalysis as "a dynamic conception which reduces mental life to the interplay of reciprocally urging and checking forces." The urging forces are *cathexes,* the checking forces are *anti-cathexes.*

As we have seen, the id has only cathexes while the ego and superego also possess anti-cathexes. In fact, the ego and superego come into existence because it is necessary to check the imprudent actions of the id. However, while the processes which constitute the ego and the superego act as brakes upon the id, the ego and superego also have their own driving forces.

Another way of looking at the concept of anti-cathexis is to view it as *internal frustration.* The resisting force frustrates the discharge of tension. This type of frustration is to be distinguished from another type which is called *external frustration.* In external frustration the goal object cannot be obtained for reasons over which the person has no control. A person may want food, but if there is no food in his environment or if he is prevented from getting it his hunger will remain unsatisfied. External frustration is a state of privation or deprivation, while internal frustration is a state of inner inhibition. When a person wants to do something but an external obstacle stands in his way, that is external frustration. When a person wants to do something but his ego or superego prevents him from doing it, that is internal frustration.

Freud observes that internal frustration (anti-cathexis) does not come into existence until external frustration prepares the ground for it. That is, a person has to experience privation or deprivation before he can develop inner controls. In the case of the superego, for example, the child does not develop self-discipline until he has had an opportunity to identify with the moral prohibitions of his parents. A child has to learn what is bad by being punished before he can establish inner controls over his conduct.

The concept of urging and checking forces enables us to understand why we think and act as we do. In general, if the urging forces are stronger than the checking forces, some action will take place or some idea will become conscious. If the anti-cathexes outweigh the cathexes, the action or the thought will be repressed. However, even if no anti-cathexis is present, the mental process may be so weakly charged that awareness or action will fail to occur.

Take, for example, the case of a person trying to recall something. He may not be able to remember because the memory trace is charged with an insufficient amount of energy. The trace may have a weak charge of energy because the experience did not make much of an impression upon him in the first place. Or the energy of the trace may have been drained off in the formation of new memory traces. The learning of something new usually means that something old has to be unlearned or forgotten. The reason for this is that a person has just so much psychic energy. When new investments are made, energy has to be borrowed from object-cathexes that are already established. Consequently the old memory cathexes are weakened as energy is added to the new memory cathexes.

Memory traces that have little energy to begin with or that have lost energy to other traces are said to be *forgotten*. They can be reinstated in memory by repetition of the experience. Thus when one forgets a telephone number he can recharge the memory trace by looking the number up in the telephone book. This is called refreshing one's memory.

On the other hand, one may be unable to recall something because the cathexis of the memory trace is opposed by a resistance or anti-cathexis. Such memories are said to be *repressed* rather than forgotten.

A repressed memory can be recalled either by reducing the strength of the anti-cathexis or by increasing the strength of the cathexis. Neither one is very easy to do. Usually it is found that the harder one tries to break through the repression, the stronger the resistance becomes. Special techniques, such as hypnosis or free association, are used to weaken resistances. The resistances also tend to become weaker during sleep so that we may recall something in a dream that is repressed during waking life.

Why are memories repressed? There are two principal reasons. Either the memory itself is a painful one or the memory is associated with something that is painful. For example, a person may forget the name of an acquaintance with whom he has had a painful encounter. Or he may forget the name because it is connected with something painful. In either case, the anti-cathexes serve the purpose of protecting the person from discomfort and anxiety. All of which means that it is easier to forget an appointment with the dentist than it is to forget a date to go dancing.

The reality of urging and checking forces in personality is brought home to one repeatedly. A typical example is the urge to empty the bladder which is checked by a recognition of the inappropriateness of the time and place for performing the act. Another familiar example is the impulse to trip a person which is inhibited by one's social feelings. Having something on the tip of one's tongue indicates that a repression is operating; the harder one tries to remember it the more difficult it becomes. If one turns one's attention to other matters, the resistance may be weakened and the repressed memory will pop up spontaneously into consciousness. Numerous other examples of the opposition of forces could be given. Sometimes the person is aware of the opposition while at other times all he experiences is a feeling of tension without being aware of the nature of the opposing forces.

The opposition of a cathexis by an anti-cathexis is called an *inner* or *endopsychic conflict*. An endopsychic conflict is one that resides within the personality. Such conflicts are to be distinguished from conflicts between the person and his environment. Although there are innumerable endopsychic conflicts, as many as there are opposing cathexes and anti-cathexes, they may all be classified under one of two categories, id-ego conflicts and ego-superego conflicts. There are no id-superego conflicts as such because the opposition between id and superego always involves the ego. That is, the id and superego come into conflict because each of them tries to use the ego for its own purposes. Moreover, a simple id-ego conflict may become complicated if the superego joins forces with the id against the ego or with the ego against the id. The ego is the common element in all conflicts, including those that involve opposition with the external world. Since the outcome of a conflict is decisive for the development of personality, we will take up this important subject again in the next chapter.

Practically every process of the personality is regulated by the interplay of cathexis and anti-cathexis. Sometimes the balance between them is so delicate that a very slight shift in the ratio of the strength of the cathexis to the strength of the anti-cathexis will mean the difference between doing and not doing something. A slight increase of cathexis or a slight decrease of anti-cathexis when a person's finger is on the trigger of a gun may cause the gun to be fired, a person to be killed, and a murderer to be tried, convicted, and hanged. The delicate balance of power which often exists between the driving and restraining forces of personality makes it extremely difficult to predict precisely what any person will do in any given situation. For just as a spark may set off a disastrous conflagration so may an almost imperceptible rise in the cathexis level initiate a far-reaching chain of events in the life of a person and in society. This inability to predict the behavior of a person prevents psychology from being a very exact science. Freud had this in mind when he wrote:

> So long as we trace the development from its final stage backwards, the connection appears continuous, and we feel we have gained an insight which is completely satisfactory or even exhaustive. But if we proceed the reverse way, if we start from the premises inferred from the analysis and try to follow these up to the final result, then we no longer get the impression of an inevitable sequence of events which could not be otherwise determined. We notice at once that there might have been another result, and that we might have been just as well able to understand and explain the latter. The synthesis is thus not so satisfactory as the analysis; in other words from a knowledge of the premises we could not have foretold the nature of the result.
>
> It is very easy to account for this disturbing state of affairs. Even supposing that we thoroughly know the aetiological factors that decide a given result, still we know them only qualitatively, and not in their relative strength. Some of them are so weak as to become suppressed by others, and therefore do not affect the final result. But we never know beforehand which of the determining factors will prove the weaker or the stronger. We only say at the end that those which succeeded must have been the stronger. Hence it is always possible by analysis to recognize the causation with certainty, whereas a prediction of it by synthesis is impossible.*

What Freud is saying here is that because of the subtleties in the relative intensities of excitatory and inhibitory forces and because small changes in the intensities may produce large effects, psychology cannot be a predictive science. It can, however, be a postdictive science in the sense that given a result it can look back

* Sigmund Freud, "The Psychogenesis of a Case of Homosexuality in a Woman." In *Collected Papers,* II (London, 1933), 226-27.

and unearth the causes that produced the result.

In the next chapter we shall return to the question of the role that cathexis and anti-cathexis play in the development of personality. We shall also examine the problem of how a cathexis can evade a resistance by finding another outlet.

V. CONSCIOUSNESS AND UNCONSCIOUSNESS

In the early years of psychoanalysis the central concept of Freud's theory was the *unconscious*. In Freud's later formulations, beginning about 1920, the unconscious was demoted from its status as the largest and most important region of the mind to the lesser status of being a quality of mental phenomena. Much of what had formerly been assigned to the unconscious became the id, and the structural distinction between consciousness and unconsciousness was replaced by the three-part organization of id, ego, and superego.

Although it is not our purpose here to write a history of the development of Freud's ideas in relation to the history of psychology, it can be pointed out that the waning importance of the unconscious in psychoanalysis was paralleled by the decreasing significance of the conscious mind in psychology. While nineteenth-century psychology was busy at its work of analyzing the conscious mind, psychoanalysis was engaged in explorations of the unconscious mind. Freud felt that consciousness was only a thin slice of the total mind, that like an iceberg, the larger part of it existed below the surface of awareness.

Psychologists answered Freud by saying that the notion of an unconscious mind was a contradiction in terms; the mind, by definition, was conscious. The controversy never reached a final conclusion because both psychology and psychoanalysis changed their objectives during the twentieth century. Psychology became a science of behavior, and psychoanalysis became a science of personality. At the present time there are many indications that the two sciences are drawing together to form a single science.

From our present vantage point it now appears that what Freud was trying to accomplish during the thirty years between 1890 and 1920, when the unconscious mind reigned as the sovereign concept in his psychological system, was to discover those determining forces in personality that are not directly known to the observer. Just as physics and chemistry make known that which is unknown about the nature of matter by means of experiment and demonstration, so the task of psychology for Freud was to seek out those factors in personality of which we are ignorant. This seems to be the meaning of Freud's statement that "our scientific work in psychology will consist in translating unconscious processes into conscious ones, and thus filling in the gaps in conscious perceptions."* Freud is merely acknowledging the well-known fact that the goal of all the sciences is to substitute knowledge for ignorance. For example, man is not directly aware of the process of digestion as it takes place, but the science of physiology can tell him what happens during digestion. This knowledge does not enable him to perceive (be directly aware of) his own digestive processes as they are occurring; nevertheless he knows (understands) what is taking place. In a similar manner, one is not aware of unconscious mental processes, but psychology can teach him about what is going on below the level of awareness.

For example, a person who has an accident is usually not aware that the accident may represent a desire to hurt himself. Yet this is precisely what a number of studies have shown. Or a person who has an abnormal craving for food or liquor is ordinarily not conscious of the fact that the craving may grow out of a frustrated desire for love. Yet this is often the case. Even when a person learns that there is a relationship between accident proneness and feelings of guilt or between alcoholism and frustrated

---

* Sigmund Freud, "Some Elementary Lessons in Psycho-analysis." In *Collected Papers*, V (London, 1950), 382.

love, he probably does not become directly conscious of this relationship as it exists in him.

Freud believed that if psychology were to justify itself as a science it would have to discover the unknown causes of behavior. That is why he made so much of unconscious causation or motivation in the early years of psychoanalysis. For Freud, what is unconscious is what is unknown.

Conscious and unconscious are retained in psychoanalytic theory after 1920 as qualities of mental phenomena. Whether a content of the mind is conscious or not depends upon the magnitude of the energy invested in it and the intensity of the resisting force. A person feels pain or he feels pleasure when the magnitude of the pain or pleasure exceeds a certain cathexis value which is called the *threshold* value. Likewise, he perceives an object in the world when the perceptual process is energized beyond a threshold value. Even when the cathexis exceeds the threshold, the feeling or the perception may not possess the quality of consciousness because of the inhibiting effects of an anti-cathexis which prevents it from becoming conscious.

For instance, cases are known of people who are unable to see in spite of the fact that there is nothing wrong with their visual mechanisms. They are blind because they do not want to see. This means that an inhibiting force (anti-cathexis) effectively blocks the visual cathexes. The reason why they do not want to see is that seeing is too painful for them. They are literally afraid of seeing, like a person who closes his eyes at the movies to avoid witnessing a particularly horrible scene.

Perceptions and feelings are direct experiences of something that is happening to the person at the present time. Memories and ideas, on the other hand, are mental representations of past experiences. In order for ideas or memories to become conscious, it is necessary for them to be associated with language. One cannot think or remember unless what he is thinking or remembering has been linked with words that he has seen or heard. Consequently one cannot consciously remember infantile experiences that occurred before language development began. Yet, in spite of the fact that one cannot remember early experiences, they may be of decisive importance in the development of personality.

Freud differentiated between two qualities of unconsciousness, the preconscious and the unconscious proper. A preconscious idea or memory is one which can become conscious quite easily because the resistance is weak. An unconscious thought or memory has a harder time becoming conscious because the opposing force is strong. Actually there are all degrees of unconsciousness. At one end of the scale there is the memory which can never become conscious because it has no association with language; at the other end is the memory which is on the tip of the tongue.

Since a relatively large concentration of energy in a mental process is required in order for it to have the quality of being conscious, energy for this purpose has to be diverted from other mental processes. This means that we can be conscious of only one thing at a time. However, the rapid shifting of energy from one idea, memory, perception, or feeling to another provides for a wide range of conscious awareness within a short space of time. One can think about or run over in memory a lot of things quickly because of the mobility with which psychic energy can be redistributed. The perceptual system is like a radar mechanism which rapidly scans and takes many quick pictures of the world. When the perceptual system discovers a needed object or apprehends a potential danger in the external world, it comes to rest and focuses its attention upon the object or danger. Ideas and memories are summoned from the preconscious to help the person adjust to the situation confronting him. When the danger is past or the need is satisfied, the mind turns its attention to other matters.

VI. THE INSTINCTS

It has been noted in a previous section of this chapter (see Section II, "Instinct") that an instinct is a sum of psychic energy which imparts direction to psychological processes, and that it has a source, an aim, an object, and an impetus. How many different instincts are there? There are as many as there are bodily needs, since an instinct is the mental representative of a bodily need. Freud said that the question as to the number of instincts is a matter to be determined by biological investigation.

In his final reckoning, Freud recognized two great groups of instincts, those that are in the service of *life* and those that are in the service of *death*. The ultimate goal of the death instincts is to return to the constancy of inorganic matter. Freud speculated that the death instincts were built into living matter at a time in the evolution of the earth when cosmic forces acting upon inorganic matter transmuted it into living forms. These first living things probably lived only a very short time and then returned (regressed) to their former inorganic state. Life consisted essentially of a disturbed state produced by external stimulation. When the disturbance quieted down the spark of life went out. As a result of these conditions surrounding the creation of life, a regression to the inorganic became an aim of the organic.

With the continuing evolution of the world, new forms of energy created disturbances that were longer lasting so that the span of life increased. Eventually living things acquired the power to reproduce themselves. At that point in evolution the creation of life became independent of external stimulation. Although the instinct of reproduction insured the continuity of life, the presence of a death instinct meant that no particular living thing could live forever. Its ultimate destiny was always to return to the inorganic. Freud believed that life was a roundabout way to death.

The death instincts perform their work inconspicuously. Little is known about them except that they inevitably accomplish their mission. However, the derivatives of the death instincts, of which destructiveness and aggression are among the more important, are far from being inconspicuous. A discussion of instinct derivatives will be found in Chapter 4, "The Development of Personality." Suffice it to say here that the derivative of an instinct is a driving force which has the same source and aim as the instinct from which it is derived, but differs with respect to the means by which the aim is reached. In other words, the derivative of an instinct is a substitute object-cathexis.

The life instincts are better known because their effects are more public. They are the mental representatives of all of the bodily needs whose satisfaction is necessary for survival and for propagation. The sex instincts are the most intimately studied of the life instincts and assume great importance in the psychoanalytic theory of personality. The sex instincts have their sources in various bodily zones, which are called *erogenous* zones. The mouth, the anus, and the genital organs are the chief erogenous zones. Freud thought that an erogenous zone might be a part of the body which was sensitized by chemical substances (hormones) secreted by the sex glands. The sex instincts arise independently of one another in the life of the individual, but at puberty (sexual maturity) they normally become synthesized in the service of reproduction. The sex instincts also interact with the other life instincts. The mouth is the portal for food as well as a part of the body which when suitably stimulated evokes sensual pleasure. The anus is the organ by which waste products are eliminated but it also gives pleasure when it is stimulated in certain ways. The principal derivative of the sex instincts is love. We shall have much more to say about the sex instincts and their derivatives in the next chapter.

The form of energy which is used by the life instincts is called *libido*, but no special name was ever given by Freud to the form of energy employed by the death instincts. In his earlier writings, Freud used the term "libido" to denote sexual energy; but when he revised his theory of motivation, libido was defined as the energy of all the life instincts.

The life and death instincts and their derivatives may fuse with one another, neutralize each other, or alternate with one another. An example of an instinctual fusion is sleep, since sleep is both a state of reduced tension (a partial return along the road back to the inorganic) and a time during which the life processes are being revitalized. Eating represents a fusion of a life instinct with destructiveness which is a derivative of the death instinct, since life is maintained by eating but at the same time food is being destroyed by being bitten, chewed, and swallowed. Love, a derivative of the sex instincts, often neutralizes hate, a derivative of the death instincts. Or they may alternate with one another as happens when love turns into hate or hate turns into love.

The instincts reside in the id, but they come to expression by guiding the processes of the ego and the superego. The ego is the principal agent of the life instincts. The ego serves the life instincts in two important ways. It comes into existence originally in order to obtain satisfaction for the basic bodily needs. It does this by learning to make realistic transactions with the environment. The ego also serves the life instincts by transforming the death instincts into forms that serve the ends of life instead of those of death. For example, the primary death wish in the id becomes transformed in the ego into aggression against enemies in the external world. By taking aggressive action a person protects himself from being injured or destroyed by his enemies. Aggression also helps him to overcome barriers that stand in the way of the satisfaction of his basic needs.

However when a person is aggressive he often encounters counter-aggression from authority figures and enemies. In order to avoid punishment, the person learns to identify with the aggressor. This means that he becomes aggressive against the very impulses which make him hostile toward others. In other words, he develops a superego which plays the same role in controlling his impulses as an external authority does.

The superego in its role as internalized authority then takes aggressive action against the ego whenever the ego contemplates being hostile or rebellious against an external authority figure. The sequence of events may be summarized as follows: (1) the child is aggressive toward the father, (2) the father retaliates by punishing the child,

(3) the child identifies with the punishing father, (4) the authority of the father is internalized and becomes the superego, and (5) the superego punishes the ego when it disobeys a moral rule of the superego. In an extreme form, the superego tries to destroy the ego. This is what happens, for example, when a person feels so ashamed of himself that he is driven to suicide.

Since the ego is the agent of life, the superego by striving to destroy the ego has the same aim as the original death wish in the id. That is why the superego is said to be the agent of the death instincts.

VII. ANXIETY

Anxiety is one of the most important concepts in psychoanalytic theory. It plays an important role in the development of personality as well as in the dynamics of personality functioning. Moreover, it is of central significance in Freud's theory of the neuroses and psychoses and in the treatment of these pathological conditions. The present discussion will limit itself to a consideration of the part that anxiety plays in the functioning of the normal personality.

Anxiety is a painful emotional experience which is produced by excitations in the internal organs of the body. These excitations result from internal or external stimulation and are governed by the autonomic nervous system. For example, when a person encounters a dangerous situation his heart beats faster, he breathes more rapidly, his mouth becomes dry, and the palms of his hands sweat.

Anxiety differs from other painful states, such as tension, pain, and melancholy by some specific quality of consciousness. Exactly what determines this quality is unknown. Freud thought that it might be some distinctive feature of the visceral excitations themselves. In any event, anxiety is a conscious state which can be distinguished subjectively by a person from experiences of pain, depression, melancholy, and tensions resulting from hunger, thirst, sex, and other bodily needs. Incidentally, there is no such thing as unconscious anxiety any more than there is such a thing as unconscious pain. One can be unaware of the reason for his anxiety, but he cannot be unaware of the feeling of anxiety. Anxiety that is not experienced is nonexistent.

Anxiety is synonymous with the emotion of fear. Freud preferred the term *anxiety* to that of *fear* because fear is usually thought of in the sense of being afraid of something in the external world. Freud recognized that one could be afraid of internal dangers as well as external ones. He differentiated three types of anxiety, *reality* or *objective anxiety, neurotic anxiety,* and *moral anxiety.*

These three types of anxiety do not differ among themselves in any qualitative way. They all have the single quality of being unpleasant. They differ only in respect to their sources. In reality anxiety, the source of the danger lies in the external world. One is afraid of a poisonous snake, a man with a gun, or an automobile that gets out of control. In neurotic anxiety, the threat resides in an instinctual object-choice of the id. A person is afraid of being overwhelmed by an uncontrollable urge to commit some act or think some thought which will prove harmful to himself. In moral anxiety, the source of the threat is the conscience of the superego system. One is afraid of being punished by the conscience for doing or thinking something which is contrary to the standards of the ego-ideal. To put it briefly, the three types of anxiety which the ego experiences are fear of the external world, fear of the id, and fear of the superego.

The distinction between these three types of anxiety does not mean that the person who is experiencing the anxiety is aware of its actual source. He may think that he is afraid of something in the external world when in reality his fear stems from an impulse danger or a superego threat. For instance, a person who is afraid of handling sharp knives may think that his fear is due to sharp knives being intrinsically dangerous, when in fact what frightens him is that he may become aggressive and hurt someone when he has a knife in his hand. Or a person may think that he is afraid of being on a high place because high places are objectively dangerous, when in ruth he is afraid that his conscience will seize the opportunity of his being on a high place to punish him for his sins by causing him to fall off. An anxiety state may have more than one source. It can be a blend of neurotic and objective anxiety, or of moral and objective anxiety, or of neurotic and moral anxiety. It can also be a blend of all three.

The sole function of anxiety is to act as a danger signal to the ego, so that when the signal appears in consciousness the ego may institute measures to deal with the danger. Although anxiety is painful and one might wish that it could be abolished, it serves a very necessary function by alerting a person to the presence of internal and external dangers. Being alerted, he can do something to ward off or avoid the danger. On the other hand, if the danger cannot be averted, anxiety may pile up and finally overwhelm the person. When this happens, the person is said to have a nervous breakdown.

A. REALITY ANXIETY   Reality anxiety is a painful emotional experience resulting from a perception of danger in the external world. A danger is any condition of the environment which threatens to harm the person. The perception of danger and the arousal of anxiety may be innate in the sense that one inherits a tendency to become afraid in the presence of certain objects or environmental conditions, or it may be acquired during the person's lifetime. For example, fear of darkness could be inborn because past generations of men were constantly being endangered during the night before they had the means of making light, or it could be learned because one is more likely to have fear-arousing experiences during the night than during the day. Or it is possible that heredity and experience are co-producers of fear of darkness. Heredity might make a person susceptible to the fear while experience might transform the susceptibility into an actuality.

In any event, fears are more easily acquired during infancy and childhood when the helplessness of the immature organism prevents him from being able to cope with external dangers. The young organism is often over-whelmed by fear because his ego has not developed to the point where it can master (bind) excessive amounts of stimulation. Experiences that overpower one with anxiety are called *traumatic,* because they reduce the person to an infantile state of helplessness. The prototype of all traumatic experiences is the *birth trauma.* The newly born baby is bombarded with excessive stimulation from the world for which his protected fetal existence has not prepared him. During his early years, the child encounters many other situations with which he cannot cope, and these traumatic experiences lay the groundwork for the development of a whole network of fears. Any situation in later life which threatens to reduce the person to an infantile state of helplessness will touch off the anxiety signal. Fears are all related to and derived from early experiences of helplessness. That is why it is so important to protect the young child from traumatic experiences.

We can and do learn, however, to react effectively when the alarm of anxiety is sounded. We flee from the danger or we do something to nullify it. We also acquire the ability to anticipate danger and to take steps to ward it off before it becomes traumatic. This ability consists of being able to recognize a very slight feeling of appre-hension as the signal for something which will become more dangerous unless it is stopped. A person is con-tinually regulating his behavior on the basis of incipient feelings of apprehension. When a person is driving a car, for example, he experiences a succession of slight appre-hensions which warn him to be on the alert for possible danger.

When one can do nothing to fend off the danger, anxiety mounts to the point where the person collapses or faints. Fear has even been known to kill a person. As we will see in the next chapter, the ego has other ways of dealing with anxiety.

B. NEUROTIC ANXIETY   Neurotic anxiety is aroused by a perception of danger from the instincts. It is a fear of what might happen should the anti-cathexes of the ego fail to prevent the instinctual object-cathexes from discharging themselves in some impulsive action.

Neurotic anxiety can be displayed in three forms. There is a free-floating type of apprehensiveness which readily attaches itself to any more or less suitable environmental circumstance. This kind of anxiety characterizes the nervous person who is always expecting something dreadful to happen. We say of such a person that he is afraid of his own shadow. We might better say that he is afraid of his own id. What he is actually afraid of is that the id which is constantly exerting pressure upon the ego will seize control of the ego and reduce it to a state of helplessness.

Another observable form of neurotic anxiety is an intense, irrational fear. This is called a *phobia*. The characteristic feature of a phobia is that the intensity of the fear is out of all proportion to the actual danger of the object of which the person is afraid. He may be deathly afraid of moths, mice, high places, crowds, open spaces, buttons, rubber, crossing the street, talking before a group, water, or light bulbs, to name only a few of the many phobias that have been reported. In each of these cases the fear is irrational because the mainspring of the anxiety is found in the id rather than in the external world. The object of the phobia represents a temptation to instinctual gratification or is associated in some way with an instinctual object-choice. Behind every neurotic fear there is a primitive wish of the id for the object of which one is afraid. The person wants what he fears or he wants something that is associated with, or symbolized by, the feared object.

For example, a young woman was deathly afraid of touching anything made of rubber. She did not know why she had this fear; she only knew that she had had it as long as she could remember. Analysis brought out the following facts. When she was a little girl, her father had brought home two balloons, one for her and one for her younger sister. In a fit of temper she broke her sister's balloon, for which she was severely punished by the father. Moreover, she had to give her sister her balloon. Upon further analysis it was learned that she had been very jealous of her younger sister, so much so that she secretly wished her sister might die and leave her the sole object of her father's devotion. The breaking of her sister's balloon signified a destructive act against her sister. The ensuing punishment and her own guilt feelings became associated with the rubber balloon. Whenever she came into contact with rubber, the old fear of the wish to destroy her sister made her shrink away.

Phobias may also be augmented by moral anxiety when the desired but feared object is one that transgresses an ideal of the superego. For example, a woman may have an irrational fear of being raped because she really wants to be sexually attacked but her superego rebels against the wish. She is really not afraid of being raped; in fact she wants to be. She is afraid of her own conscience for harboring the wish. In other words, one part of her personality is at war with another part. The id says, "I want it"; the superego says, "How horrible"; and the ego says, "I am afraid." This is the explanation for many strong fears.

The third form of neurotic anxiety is observed in panic or near-panic reactions. These reactions appear suddenly and with no apparent provocation. One reads occasionally about someone running berserk and shooting down a lot of people whom he does not even know and who have not done anything to him. Subsequently he cannot explain why he did such a thing. All he knows is that he felt so upset and so tense that he had to do something before he exploded. These panic reactions are examples of discharge behavior which aims to rid the person of excessively painful neurotic anxiety by doing that which the id demands, in spite of ego and superego prohibitions.

Panic behavior is an extreme form of a reaction which is often displayed in less violent forms. It is seen whenever a person does something that is out of character with his usual behavior. It may be blurting out a particularly offensive word, taking an article of little value from a store, or making an insulting remark about someone. In such cases the person is said to be acting out his impulses. Acting out one's impulses reduces neurotic anxiety by relieving the pressure which the id exerts upon the ego.

Needless to say, acting-out behavior will result in an increase of reality anxiety when the impulsive act evokes a threatening reaction from the environment, as it usually does. A child is repeatedly being punished for acting on impulse, so that he usually learns to control his impulses. If he does not learn control as a child and grows up to be an impulsive person, society has provisions for dealing with him through legal channels. Even so, law-abiding citizens have been known to break the law under the pressure of neurotic anxiety. Their controls break down and their impulses rush out into behavior. Although well-controlled people usually regret impulsive actions and emotional outbursts, there is a sense of relief that comes from exploding.

Neurotic anxiety is based upon reality anxiety in the sense that a person has to associate an instinctual demand with an external danger before he learns to fear his instincts. As long as instinctual discharge does not result in punishment, one has nothing to fear from instinctual object-cathexes. However, when impulsive behavior gets the person into trouble, as it usually does, he learns how dangerous the instincts are. Slaps and spankings and other forms of punishment show the child that impulsive instinctual gratification leads to a state of discomfort. The child acquires neurotic anxiety when he is punished for being impulsive.

Neurotic anxiety can be much more of a burden upon the ego than objective anxiety is. As we grow older we develop ways of mastering or avoiding external threats, and even as children we can always flee from dangerous objects or situations. But since the source of neurotic anxiety is a province of one's own personality, it is much harder to deal with it and quite impossible to flee from it. The development of personality, as we shall see in the next chapter, is determined in large measure by the kinds of adaptations and mechanisms which are formed in the ego to deal with neurotic and moral anxiety. The fight against fears is one of the decisive engagements in psychological growth, the outcome of which bears so heavily upon the final character of the person.

Before this section is brought to a close the reader should take note that neurotic anxiety is not something that is the exclusive possession of neurotic people. Normal people experience neurotic anxiety, too, but it does not control their lives to the same extent that it controls the lives of neurotics. After all, the difference between a neurotic person and a normal person is one of degree, and the borderline between the two is a shadowy one.

C. MORAL ANXIETY

Moral anxiety, which is experienced as feelings of guilt or shame in the ego, is aroused by a perception of danger from the conscience. The conscience as the internalized agent of parental authority threatens to punish the person for doing something or thinking something which transgresses the perfectionistic aims of the ego-ideal that have been laid down in the personality by the parents. The original fear from which moral anxiety is derived is an objective one; it is fear of the punitive parents. As is the case with neurotic anxiety, the source of moral anxiety lies within the personality structure, and as with neurotic anxiety the person cannot escape from feelings of guilt by running away from them. The conflict is purely *intrapsychic,* which means that it is a structural one and does not involve a relationship between the person and the world, except in the historical sense that moral anxiety is an outgrowth of an objective fear of the parents.

Moral anxiety has close ties with neurotic anxiety since the chief enemies of the superego are the primitive object-choices of the id. These ties result from the discipline of parents which is largely directed against expressions of sexual and aggressive impulses. As a consequence, the conscience, which is the internalized voice of parental authority, consists of prohibitions against sensuality and disobedience.

It is one of the ironies of life that a virtuous person experiences more shame than an unvirtuous person does. The reason for this is that merely thinking of doing something bad makes a virtuous person feel ashamed. A person who exercises a lot of self-control is bound to give a good deal of thought to instinctual temptations since he does not find other outlets for his instinctual urges. A less virtuous person does not have as strong a superego, so that he is less likely to feel conscience-stricken when he thinks or does something that is alien to the moral code. Guilt feelings are a part of the price the idealistic person pays for instinctual renunciation.

We have said that anxiety is a warning to the ego that it is in peril. In objective anxiety if the person does not heed the warning something harmful happens to him. He suffers a physical injury or pain, or he experiences privation or deprivation. By paying attention to the warning, a person may be able to avoid harm. In both neurotic and moral anxiety the peril does not lie in the external world nor is it some painful physical injury or physical privation that the person fears. What then does he fear? He is afraid of fear itself. This is clearly apparent in the case of guilt feelings which are directly painful to the person. They may become so unbearable, in fact, that the guilty person may do something to invite punishment from an external source in order to expiate his guilt and secure relief. People have been known to commit crimes out of a sense of guilt. They are easily caught because they want to be caught and punished. In a similar manner, the increasing pressure of neurotic anxiety may cause a person to lose his head and do something very impulsive. The consequences of the impulsive deed are reckoned as being less painful than the anxiety itself. Neurotic and moral anxiety is not only a signal of impending danger to the ego, it is also the danger itself.

VIII. SUMMARY

In this chapter, we have been concerned with the personality as a complex and intricate energy system. The form of energy that operates the personality and enables it to perform work is called *psychic energy*. Where does this energy come from? It comes from the vital energy of the body. Vital energy is transformed into psychic energy. How this transformation takes place is not known.

The reservoir of psychic energy is the id. The energy of the id is used to gratify the basic life and death instincts. By means of the mechanism of *identification*, energy is withdrawn from the reservoir and is used to activate the ego and the superego.

The energy at the disposal of the ego and the superego is employed for two general purposes. It either helps to discharge tension by being invested in *cathexes,* or it prevents the discharge of tension by being invested in *anti-cathexes*. Anti-cathexes are established primarily for the purpose of reducing anxiety and avoiding pain. What a person thinks and what he does are determined by the relative strengths of these driving and resisting forces.

In the final analysis, the dynamics of personality consists of the exchanges of psychic energy among the three systems of personality.

REFERENCES

Energy, Instinct, and Cathexis

FREUD, SIGMUND. (1915.) "Instincts and Their Vicissitudes." In *Collected Papers*, Vol. IV, pp. 60-83. London: The Hogarth Press, 1946.

FREUD, SIGMUND. (1920.) *Beyond the Pleasure Principle*. London: The Hogarth Press, 1948.

FREUD, SIGMUND. (1923.) *The Ego and the Id*, Chap. IV. London: The Hogarth Press, 1947.

FREUD, SIGMUND. (1924.) "The Economic Problem in Masochism." In *Collected Papers*, Vol. II, pp. 255-68. London: The Hogarth Press, 1933.

FREUD, SIGMUND. (1933.) *New Introductory Lectures on Psycho-analysis*, Chap. 4. New York: W. W. Norton & Company, Inc., 1933.

FREUD, SIGMUND. (1938.) *An Outline of Psychoanalysis*, Chap. 2. New York: W. W. Norton & Company, Inc., 1949.

Consciousness and Unconsciousness

FREUD, SIGMUND. (1900.) *The Interpretation of Dreams*, Chap. 7. London: The Hogarth Press, 1953.

FREUD, SIGMUND. (1912.) "A Note on the Unconscious in Psycho-analysis." In *Collected Papers*, Vol. IV, pp. 22-29. London: The Hogarth Press, 1946.

FREUD, SIGMUND. (1915.) "The Unconscious." In *Collected Papers*, Vol. IV, pp. 98-136. London: The Hogarth Press, 1946.

FREUD, SIGMUND. (1923.) *The Ego and the Id*, Chap. I. London: The Hogarth Press, 1947.

FREUD, SIGMUND. (1938.) *An Outline of Psychoanalysis*, Chap. 4. New York: W. W. Norton & Company, Inc., 1949.

Anxiety

FREUD, SIGMUND. (1926.) *Inhibitions, Symptoms and Anxiety*. London: The Hogarth Press, 1948.

FREUD, SIGMUND. (1933.) *New Introductory Lectures on Psycho-analysis*, Chap. 4. New York: W. W. Norton & Company, Inc., 1933.

CHAPTER FOUR

The Development of Personality

One of the obvious facts about personality is that it is constantly changing and developing. This is especially noticeable during the periods of infancy, childhood, and adolescence. Structurally, the ego becomes more differentiated and, dynamically, it secures increasing control over the instinctual sources of energy. There is an elaboration of behavior patterns, a proliferation of object-cathexes in the form of interests and attachments, and a development of the psychological processes of perception, memory, and thinking. The whole personality becomes more integrated, which means that energy exchanges between the three systems and with the external world are facilitated. Cathexes and anti-cathexes tend to become stabilized as the person grows older, so that the personality functions in a smoother, more orderly, and more consistent fashion. Through learning, one develops greater skill in dealing with frustrations and anxieties. These and many other changes in the person are the result of five major conditions: (1) maturation, (2) painful excitations resulting from external privations and deprivations (external frustration), (3) painful excitations arising from internal conflicts (cathexes versus anti-cathexes), (4) personal inadequacies, and (5) anxiety.

Maturation consists of innately controlled sequences of developmental changes. Walking is an example of a maturational process. At first, the baby has no power of locomotion; then, as a result of the growth of bones, muscles and tendons, and developments within the nervous system, the baby goes through a well-defined series of progressions beginning with the lifting of the head and eventuating in the taking of his first steps by himself. Language development displays a similar set of progressions from the babbling of the baby to the meaningful verbalizations of the child. Perception, memory, learning, judgment, and thought are influenced by the maturation of the central nervous system, and the instincts, notably the sexual instinct, are altered by the maturation of the neuro-humoral system consisting of the autonomic nervous system and the endocrine glands. Maturation is pervasive. There is probably no aspect of development that does not bear its imprint; yet it is difficult if not impossible to disentangle the effects of maturation from those of learning. Maturation and learning go hand in hand in the development of personality.

A frustration is anything that prevents a painful or uncomfortable excitation from being discharged. In other words, a frustration is something that stands in the way of the operation of the pleasure principle. The person may be frustrated because the necessary goal object is not to be found in the environment. This is called *privation*. Or the goal object may be present but it is withheld or taken away from the person who wants it. This is called *deprivation*. Privation and deprivation are classified as external frustrations because they reside in the environment.

Frustration may also be due to something within the person. There may be an opposing force or anti-cathexis which prevents the person from obtaining satisfaction. This is called a *conflict*. Or the person may lack the necessary skill, understanding, intelligence, or experience to make a satisfactory adjustment. These weaknesses or limitations that lie within the person are called *personal inadequacies*. Finally, frustration may be due to fear. The person is afraid to go after the things that he wants. The fear may be real, neurotic, or moral, or some combination of these.

The ways in which a person meets and attempts to overcome or adjust to these obstacles shape his personality. This is the subject matter of the present chapter.

We turn now to consider some of the principal methods by which a person tries to resolve his frustrations, conflicts, and anxieties. These methods are identification, displacement, sublimation, defense mechanisms, and the transformation of instincts by fusion and compromise.

I. IDENTIFICATION

In the preceding chapter, the formation of the ego and the superego was accounted for by the mechanism of *identification*. It was said that the ego and the superego attract energy away from the id by making ideational and moralistic identifications with the instinctual object-choices of the id. At this time we wish to discuss more fully the nature of identification and its role in personality development.

In the present context, identification will be defined as the incorporation of the qualities of an external object, usually those of another person, into one's personality. A person who successfully identifies with another person will resemble that person. One of the reasons why children resemble their parents is that they assimilate the characteristics of their parents. The tendency to copy and imitate other people is an important factor in molding personality.

Under what conditions does identification take place? There are at least four important ones. The first has very little to do with frustration and anxiety. It depends solely upon the spread of narcissistic cathexis (self-love) to those features of another person which are cathected in one's self. For example, a boy who cathects his own masculine features will be more likely to value the masculine features of other males, not because he wants to possess them but because they are like his. We always tend to identify with people who have the same characteristics that we have. This applies to material possessions as well as to personal traits. A person who owns a Cadillac is more likely to identify with other people who own Cadillacs than with those who own Fords. This type of identification is called *narcissistic identification*.

Narcissism is Freud's term for self-love. It is taken from the myth of Narcissus, who fell in love with his own image which he saw reflected in a pool of water. We say a person is narcissistic when he spends a lot of time admiring himself.

Narcissistic identification should not be confused with object-choice. When a person makes an object-choice he does so because he wants the object. In narcissistic identification the person already has the object he wants; his cathexis merely fans out to include other people who have the same object. Men identify with other men because they share certain common characteristics, but they cathect women because women are a means by which tensions of various kinds can be reduced.

If the factor of narcissism is very strong, a person may derive satisfaction only from choosing a love object who resembles himself. This is one reason why a person may choose homosexuality in preference to heterosexuality, or why a man may marry a masculine woman or a woman marry a feminine man. One loves the reflected image of himself as Narcissus did.

It is quite possible that all object-choices are influenced to some degree by narcissism. Two people, for example, will usually not fall in love unless they resemble one another in some way. In general, people of the same social class and with similar interests and tastes fall in love and get married.

Narcissistic identification is responsible for the ties that exist between members of the same group. Members of a fraternity identify with one another because they all share at least one common characteristic: membership in the same organization. Whenever two or more people have something in common, whether it be a physical or mental trait, an interest, a value, a possession, membership in the same club, citizenship, or whatever, they tend to identify with one another. Two people may identify with one another because they both want the same thing, yet fight with each other over possession of the desired object. It may sound paradoxical to speak of an affinity between enemies or rivals, but there can be no doubt that such affinities do exist. Enemies sometimes become friends, and competition sometimes turns into co-operation. The policeman identifies with the thief, and the thief with the policeman.

A second type of identification grows out of frustration and anxiety. Consider, for example, the plight of a girl who wants to be loved. She sees her friends falling in love and wonders what they have that she is lacking. She decides to imitate her friends, hoping thereby to achieve the same goal they have. This type of identification, in which a frustrated person identifies with a successful person in order to be successful himself, is called *goal-oriented identification*.

Goal-oriented identifications are very common and have a great effect upon the development of personality. A boy grows to be more and more like his father if the father is achieving goals that the boy also desires. A girl will identify with her mother for the same reason and with the same result. On the other hand, if the father or mother are not pursuing goals desired by the child, the child will look elsewhere for suitable models. One of the reasons why movies are so popular is that the spectator can identify with the successful hero or heroine, or with the villain if he chooses, and vicariously satisfy his own frustrated wishes. By vicarious satisfaction is meant that the person himself does not reach the goal but he is identified with someone who does. If one cannot be famous himself he may derive satisfaction merely from being associated with a famous person.

It should be emphasized that goal-oriented identifications are usually with individual qualities of another person and not necessarily with the whole person. A boy may identify with his father's strength and not with his interests in reading and golf, because it is strength that the son considers important and not the father's recreational activities. However, identifications tend to generalize. This means that if a person identifies with some traits possessed by another person he will be likely to identify with other traits as well. Moreover, it may be difficult to isolate precisely those characteristics which make another person successful; consequently, a total rather than a partial identification will be made.

When a person has lost or cannot possess a cathected object, he may attempt to recover or secure it by making himself like the object. This type of identification may be called *object-loss identification*.

Object-loss identification is common among children who have been rejected by their parents. They try to regain parental love by behaving in accordance with the expectations of the parents. A child will identify with what he thinks the parents want him to be. Or a person who has lost a parent by separation or death may resolve to model his character upon the ideals of the missing parent. In these examples we see that it is not necessarily the actual character of the parents which determines the kind of identification made by the child; rather the child assimilates the standards and values of the parents. This is the way in which the ego-ideal is formed.

Object-loss identification may serve to restore the actual object. By being good the child actually regains parental affection. Or it may serve to take the place of the lost object. If one adopts the characteristics of the missing person that person becomes thereby a part of one's personality. The personality in the course of development becomes stamped with the imprint of many lost object-cathexes.

The fourth type of identification is one in which a person identifies with the prohibitions laid down by an authority figure. The purpose of this kind of identification is to enable one to avoid punishment by being obedient to the demands of a potential enemy. One identifies out of fear rather than out of love. Such identifications are the foundation upon which the conscience is based. The network of restraining forces which constitutes the conscience represents the incorporation of parental restraints. By regulating his behavior through self-imposed restraints (anti-cathexes), the child avoids doing those things for which he would be punished. As the child grows older, similar identifications are made with the demands of other dominant people.

By identifying with authority figures, the child becomes socialized. This means that he learns to submit to the rules and regulations of the society in which he lives. By submitting to these rules, he avoids pain and obtains pleasure. The stability of society is based largely upon the identifications that the younger generation makes with the ideals and prohibitions of the older and dominant generation. The younger generation may rebel against convention but they usually end up by conforming to society.

Before leaving this topic we might mention a very primitive form of identification. This consists of eating something in order to become like the thing eaten. For example, a native hunter eats the heart of a lion that he has killed in order to become as brave as a lion. This primitive type of identification persists symbolically in the Christian sacrament. By eating the wafer and drinking the wine which are symbols of the body and blood of Christ, the person is supposed to become more Christlike.

We have seen in this section how identification shapes the personality by producing resemblances between a person and the characteristics of objects, usually other people, in the external world. The motive force for identification, aside from the narcissistic variety, is provided by frustration, inadequacy, and anxiety, and the purpose served by identification is the discharge of painful tension through mastery of the frustration, inadequacy, or anxiety. Four types of identification were discussed (1) *narcissistic,* which is defined as the spread of self-cathexis to other people and things that resemble the self, (2) *goal-oriented,* which is defined as the modeling of one's personality upon that of a person who is achieving goals the identifier would like to achieve, (3) *object-loss,* which is defined as the incorporation of cathected objects that one has lost or not been able to possess, and (4) *with an aggressor,* which is defined as the incorporation of prohibitions imposed by an authority figure.

II. DISPLACEMENT AND SUBLIMATION

In the discussion of instincts in Chapter 3 it was pointed out that the most variable feature of an instinct is the object or means by which the aim of the instinct, i.e., reduction of tension, is achieved. If one object is not available the cathexis can shift from it to one that is available. This means that psychological energy has the property of being displaceable. The process by which energy is rechanneled from one object to another object is called *displacement*. The development of personality proceeds, in large measure, by a series of energy displacements or object substitutions. The source and aim of the instinct remain the same when energy is displaced; it is only the goal object that varies.

The causes of displacement are the same as those that produce all personality development, namely, maturation, frustration, conflict, inadequacy, and anxiety. Consider, for instance, the series of displacements that occur in the case of what is called oral gratification. The mouth and lips are sensitive zones which are intimately associated with the act of eating. The stimulation of the lips by a nipple causes the baby to suck. Although sucking serves the purpose of hunger satisfaction, the gentle stimulation of the lips is pleasurable in its own right and the lack of such stimulation after a period of time is irritating. There is, in other words, a need to suck which if it is not fully satisfied by the ingestion of food will express itself in other ways. The baby will suck its own fingers or other objects within reach. If he is punished for sucking his thumb, the child will discover or be given other objects, e.g., a candy sucker, which he can suck without fear of being punished. As he grows older, childish forms of lip stimulation are abandoned under social pressure and adult ways are adopted. Smoking, kissing, wetting the lips with the tongue, applying lipstick, drinking, whistling, singing, talking, chewing gum and tobacco, and spitting are some of the oral activities engaged in by adults.

This does not mean that these substitute object-cathexes depend solely upon the rechanneling of instinctual sucking and hunger energy. Other instincts may also find some satisfaction in the oral habit at the same time that localized oral tensions are being reduced. Kissing is also sexually gratifying and the drinking of alcoholic beverages may reduce many tensions in addition to those in the lips. As a matter of fact, it is characteristic of adult object-choices that they are determined by a confluence of energy from many vital sources. This is known as the *fusion of instincts*. Adult interests and preferences, unlike those of children, are complexly motivated, or as Freud expressed it, they are *overdetermined*. By overdetermination is meant that any given object-choice might satisfy a multiplicity of instincts. Instinct fusions and overdetermination are also known as *condensations*. The channeling of several instincts upon an object represents a condensation of energy sources. An activity like gardening or a hobby like making model airplanes can reduce simultaneously a number of more or less unrelated tensions. One reason for the persistent, unflagging, enduring interest of an adult in his work or in a hobby is this factor of multiple-channeled motivation. A child quickly tires of what he is doing because each activity is an expression of only one, or at the most a few, motives which are rapidly satisfied.

What determines the direction that a displacement will take? Why is one object rather than another selected as a substitute for the original object-choice? Why does one person develop one set of interests and attachments and another person a different set of interests and attachments? Why do interests and attachments change during one's life?

There are two major reasons why displacements follow a particular course. First, society, acting through its principal agents, the parents, influences the direction of displacement by sanctioning certain object-choices and prohibiting others. In childhood, thumbsucking is ordinarily condemned while licking a lollipop is condoned. Adults who lick lollipops are apt to be ridiculed, but society permits and may even encourage them to suck on a cigarette, a cigar, or a pipe. An adult who sucked on the nipple of a baby's bottle would be the object of scorn and contempt, but he can drink beer from a bottle with impunity. Society places restrictions upon certain kinds of object-choices but it also usually offers satisfying substitutes. When society fails to provide suitable substitutes, people tend to use the forbidden objects anyway. Witness the response that was made to the prohibition of the manufacture and sale of alcoholic beverages in the United States during the 1920's. Bootleggers and speakeasies flourished because people would not be denied this form of oral gratification.

The second important determiner of the direction that displacement takes is the degree of resemblance between the original and substitute object, or what amounts to the same thing, the extent to which the objects are identified with one another. If a person is barred from discharging tension by one route, he will seek another outlet which is as much like the forbidden path as it is possible for it to be. If this outlet is also frustrated he will look for a third object, and so forth until he finds one he can have. The degree of resemblance usually becomes less and less with each successive displacement so that the final choice may be quite different from and therefore much less satisfying than the original object. When it is said that one object is less satisfying than another, it means that the outcome of the transaction with the object yields less tension-reduction. In other words, commerce with a substitute object leaves the person with residual or undischarged tension. His final choice represents a compromise; the substitute object is better than nothing but less gratifying than the original choice. The ego which controls the final object selection has to make many such compromises between the conflicting demands of the id, the superego, and the external world.

A series of displacements in which each successive substitution is less closely identified with the original choice may be illustrated by the following example. A boy's first love object is ordinarily his mother. She is originally perceived as the ideal woman. Because it is impossible for him to obtain exclusive possession of his mother and because he discovers that she has imperfections, he is motivated to look for a substitute who is both perfect and available. The choice may fall upon his first-grade teacher or a next-door neighbor or an aunt until he finds out that they also have their drawbacks or are not available. Next he falls in love with an older girl, perhaps an older sister or the girl friend of an older brother or his father's secretary. These choices turn out to be blind alleys. He may start daydreaming about the perfect woman or try to find her in the movies or in books. If he has talent he may write poetry or paint pictures which embody his conception of the ideal woman. In the end he usually settles for a real person, a person who resembles his mother or an idealized version of his mother. In this search for a mother substitute, displacement is piled upon displacement so that a whole network of object-cathexes is constructed. The energy from a blocked cathexis distributes itself among many new activities just as a dammed-up river overflows into many new channels. His interests, hobbies, personal habits and traits, values, attitudes, sentiments, and attachments may all be colored by the displacement of energy from the frustrated desire to obtain exclusive possession of the ideal mother.

When the substitute object is one that represents a higher cultural goal, this type of displacement is called a *sublimation*. Examples of sublimation are the deflection of energy into intellectual, humanitarian, cultural, and artistic pursuits. The direct expression of sexual and aggressive instincts is transformed into apparently non-sexual and non-aggressive forms of behavior. The source and aim of the instinctual energy remains the same in sublimated activities, as it does in all displacements, but the object or means by which the tensions are reduced changes. Freud observed that da Vinci's interest in painting Madonnas was a sublimated expression of a longing for his mother from whom he had been separated at an early age. Shakespeare's sonnets, Walt Whitman's poetry, Tschaikowsky's music, and Proust's great novel have all been regarded in some quarters as sublimated expressions of their homosexual yearnings. Since they could not obtain complete satisfaction for their sexual cravings in real life, they turned to imaginative creations. Less talented people, who have just as much need to sublimate as great artists and writers, employ more commonplace diversions for their instinctual energies. Freud points out that the development of civilization is made possible by the inhibition of primitive object-cathexes. The energy which is prevented from discharging itself in direct ways is diverted into socially useful and culturally creative channels. Sublimation does not result in complete satisfaction; there is always some residual tension which cannot be discharged by sublimated object-choices. This tension is responsible, in part, for the nervousness of civilized man, but it is also responsible for the highest achievements of mankind.

Freud points out that a person never actually relinquishes his original object-cathexis. By this he means that a person is always looking for his first love in the substitute object. Failing to find a completely satisfactory substitute, he either continues his search or reconciles himself to something that is second best. When a person accepts a substitute he is said to be *compensating* for the original goal object. A short person who wants to be tall may compensate by "acting big," a person who wants to be loved may compensate by drinking or overeating; an unmarried woman whose desire for children is frustrated may compensate by becoming a teacher. The character structure contains many such compensations; in fact, most adult interests and attachments are compensations for frustrated infantile and childish wishes. This does not mean that the compensations themselves are infantile; it means that the sources of energy upon which the compensations depend for their existence are derived from the displacement of energy from early object-choices.

A lawyer may get a great deal of oral gratification from arguing a case before a jury, a surgeon may find an outlet for his aggressive urges by operating upon patients, and a psychologist may be satisfying childish desires for sexual information by pursuing scientific studies of sexual behavior, yet it could hardly be said that the professional activities of the lawyer, surgeon, or psychologist were childish and immature. It is the way in which the energy is used that differentiates the child from the adult, not the sources of the energy or the final aims, which are pretty much the same at all age levels. The lawyer may reduce almost as much oral tension by presenting a case to the jury as the child does by sucking a stick of candy, but the means by which they secure relief are entirely different. A person who devotes his life to investigating sex behavior may get almost as much relief from sexual tensions as the Don Juan who practices what the scientist studies, yet the results of their activities are hardly the same. One adds to knowledge while the other merely obtains sensual pleasure.

The ability to displace energy from one object to another is the most powerful instrumentality for the development of personality. As we saw in the preceding chapter, the formation of the ego and the superego is accomplished by the displacement of large amounts of energy from id processes to processes which make up the ego and the superego. The further development of the ego and the superego is brought about to a large extent by displacements of energy within each system. The whole complex network of adult interests, preferences, values, attitudes, and attachments, and the acquisition and abandonment of them throughout life, are made possible by displacement. If psychological energy were not displaceable and distributive there could be no development of personality.

When it is said that psychic energy is distributive it means that the energy can be parceled out among a number of activities. The same energy source can perform many different kinds of work, just as the electricity flowing into one's house can be used to toast bread, mix a cake, run a vacuum cleaner, or shave one's beard. The energy of the sexual instinct, for example, can be distributed among such diverse activities as gardening, writing a letter, attending a baseball game, or daydreaming.

III. DEFENSE MECHANISMS OF THE EGO

One of the major tasks imposed upon the ego is that of dealing with the threats and dangers that beset the person and arouse anxiety. The ego may try to master danger by adopting realistic problem-solving methods, or it may attempt to alleviate anxiety by using methods that deny, falsify, or distort reality and that impede the development of personality. The latter methods are called *defense mechanisms* of the ego. There are a number of these mechanisms, the most important of which will be described in this section.

A. REPRESSION A cathexis of the id, ego, or superego which produces anxiety may be prevented from registering itself in consciousness by being opposed by an anti-cathexis. The nullifying or restraining of a cathexis by an anti-cathexis is called *repression*.

There are two kinds of repression, *primal repression* and *repression proper*. Primal repression prevents an instinctual object-choice which has never been conscious from becoming conscious. Primal repressions are innately determined barriers which are responsible for keeping a large part of the contents of the id permanently unconscious. These primal repressions have been built into the person as a result of racial experience with painful situations. For example, the taboo against incest is said to be based upon a strong desire for sexual relations with one's father or mother. The expression of this desire is punished by the parents. When this happens over and over again during the racial history of mankind, the repression of the incestuous desire is built into man and becomes a primal repression. This means that each new generation does not have to learn to repress the desire since the repression itself is inherited.

Incidentally, a strong taboo such as the incest taboo signifies a strong desire for the prohibited object. Otherwise, there would be no need for a strong prohibition.

By being kept out of awareness, dangerous instinctual object-choices are unable to evoke anxiety on the principle that what we don't know can't hurt us. However, these object-choices may affect behavior in various indirect ways or associate themselves with material which does become conscious, thereby arousing anxiety. The ego may then deal with the disguised penetration of threatening id-cathexes into consciousness or behavior by instituting repression proper. Repression proper (hereafter called simply *repression*) forces a dangerous memory, idea, or perception out of consciousness and sets up a barrier against any form of motor discharge.

For example, repression may prevent a person from seeing something that is in plain view, or distort that which he does see, or falsify the information coming in through the sense organs, in order to protect the ego from apprehending an object that is dangerous or that is associated with a danger that would arouse anxiety. Similarly, repression operates upon memories that are traumatic or upon memories that are associated with a traumatic experience. The associated memories may be perfectly harmless in themselves, but by recalling them the person runs the risk of remembering the traumatic experience as well. Therefore a whole complex of memories may fall under the influence of repression. Dangerous ideas may also be repressed. In every case, whether it be a perception, a memory, or an idea that is repressed, the purpose is to abolish objective, neurotic, or moralistic anxiety by denying or falsifying the existence of the external or internal threat to the ego's safety.

Although repression is necessary for normal personality development and is used to some extent by everyone, there are people who depend upon it to the exclusion of other ways of adjusting to threats. These people are said to be repressed. Their contacts with the world are limited and they give the impression of being withdrawn, tense, rigid, and guarded. Their lips are set and their movements are wooden. They use so much of their energy in maintaining their far-flung repressions that they do not have very much left over for pleasurable and productive interactions with the environment and with other people.

Sometimes repression will interfere with the normal

functioning of a part of the body. A repressed person may be sexually impotent or frigid because he is afraid of the sex impulse, or he may develop what is called hysterical blindness or hysterical paralysis. In hysterical blindness or paralysis, the eyes and muscles are perfectly sound but the anti-cathexes prevent the individual from seeing or from moving a leg or an arm. The mechanism of repression contributes to the development of many physical disturbances, for example arthritis, asthma, and ulcers, which are among the most notable of the so-called psychosomatic disorders. Arthritis may arise from the inhibition of hostility. The inhibition spreads to the musculature, through which aggression is overtly expressed, and creates a condition of painful tension, which if it persists for a long time develops into a chronic arthritic condition. Similarly, asthma may be due to the spread of repression to the breathing mechanism. A state of apprehension causes a person to breathe in a light and shallow manner. Consequently, he does not get enough oxygen into his system and enough carbon dioxide out. The resulting partial asphyxiation produces a gasping for breath, so characteristic of the asthmatic person. Ulcers may develop when fear interferes with the digestion.

Although the ego is the seat of repression, it may be acting under orders from the superego when it institutes a repression. Consequently, the more influential the superego is in the character structure, the more repressions there are likely to be. Repressions which are brought about by the superego are the internalized version of parental restraints imposed upon the child.

What happens to the repressed cathexes? They may exist unchanged in the personality, they may force their way through the opposing barriers, they may find expression by displacement, or the repression may be lifted. For example, the impetus of the sex instinct may increase so much during adolescence that it overwhelms the resistances established during childhood. Under strong provocation a person who has repressed his aggressive urges may become very belligerent. When the dam of repression is broken, there is customarily an intense outpouring of energy like the response of a child when he is let out of school.

Displacement permits the repressed cathexes to find some kind of more or less satisfying fulfillment. However, it is necessary for the displacement to conceal the original source of the cathexis, otherwise the ego will discover the subterfuge and invoke the mechanism of repression again. Repressed cathexes employ all manner of disguises by which to secure discharge. A child who has repressed his hostility against his father may express it as an adult in a symbolic form of breaking the law or rebelling against the conventions of society. Repressed desires often find symbolic fulfillment in dreams. Dreaming of entering a house, for instance, may symbolize an incestuous wish for the mother, if house and mother are associated together in the mind of the dreamer. Repression of the desire to punish oneself may cause a person to punish himself in indirect ways such as having accidents, losing things, and making foolish mistakes. A repressed cathexis may express itself in the form of a verbal denial of the very thing that a person really wants. "I don't want that" may actually mean "I do want it." When a person says, "That's the last thing I was thinking of," it may mean it was the first.

Repressions may be lifted when the source of the threat disappears so that the repression is no longer necessary. However, the lifting of a repression does not occur automatically. One has to discover that the danger no longer exists. He discovers this by testing reality. It is difficult to make such a test when the repression is still in place, yet the repression will not disappear until the test is made. This is why a person is apt to carry around a lot of unnecessary fears that are hangovers from childhood. He never gets a chance to discover that the fear no longer has any foundation.

Although repression is responsible for many abnormal conditions, its role in normal personality development should not be minimized. The erection of a battery of repressing forces against the instinctual object-cathexes of the id protects the infantile ego from attacks by the id and enables the ego to develop its latent resources and capacities. When the ego has acquired sufficient strength to cope with danger by more rational methods, repression is no longer necessary and its persistence constitutes a drain upon the ego's energy. The lifting of repressions as one grows older frees the energy which is invested in anti-cathexes for more productive enterprises.

B. PROJECTION   When a person is made to feel anxious by pressure upon the ego from the id or superego, he can try to relieve his anxiety by attributing its causation to the external world. Instead of saying, "I hate him," one can say, "He hates me"; or instead of saying, "My conscience is bothering me," one can say, "He is bothering me." In the first case, one denies that the hostility springs from the id and attributes it to another person. In the second case, one denies the source of the feelings of persecution and ascribes it to someone else. This type of ego defense against neurotic and moral anxiety is called *projection*.

The essential feature of projection is that the subject of the feeling, which is the person himself, is changed. It may take the form of exchanging the subject for the object. "I hate you" is converted into "You hate me." Or it may take the form of substituting one subject for another subject while the object remains the same. "I am punishing myself" is changed into "He is punishing me." What the ego is actually trying to do when it employs projection is to transform neurotic or moral anxiety into objective anxiety. A person who is afraid of his own aggressive and sexual impulses obtains some relief for his anxiety by attributing aggressiveness and sexuality to other people. They are the ones who are aggressive and sexual, not he. Likewise, a person who is afraid of his own conscience consoles himself with the thought that other people are responsible for bothering him, and that it is not his conscience.

What is the purpose of such a transformation? It serves the purpose of changing an internal danger from the id or the superego which is difficult for the ego to handle into an external danger which is easier for the ego to deal with. A person usually has more opportunity to learn how to cope with objective fears than he has to acquire skill in mastering neurotic and moral anxiety.

Projection does more than help alleviate anxiety. It also offers a person an excuse for expressing his real feelings. A person who believes that he is hated or persecuted may use this belief as a justification for attacking his imaginary enemy. By using the pretext of defending himself against his enemies he is able to gain satisfaction for his hostile impulses. He obtains pleasure without feeling guilty because he feels that his aggression is justified. Of course, the whole affair is an elaborate subterfuge or rationalization for evading personal responsibility for one's acts by blaming someone else.

The term *rationalization* is used here in the sense of finding a justifiable excuse or alibi in the external world for doing something that is frowned upon by the superego. Rationalization also refers to the substitution of a socially approved motive for a socially disapproved one. A person who gives a lot of money to charity may think he is doing it out of the kindness of his heart when he is really motivated by a desire to show off or by a guilty conscience. Obviously one cannot be conscious of projecting or rationalizing, otherwise the mechanisms would not alleviate anxiety. This is true of all the defenses of the ego; they must operate unconsciously in order to be effective in reducing anxiety.

The projection of superego prohibitions and punishments is very easily accomplished because the superego is the internal representative of something that was originally external. Before the superego was formed, prohibitions and punishments were inflicted by the parents. Consequently, that which was once external can be made external again. This is more likely to happen when the superego has not been securely incorporated into the personality structure. A person with a weakly integrated superego is more disposed to attribute his guilty feelings to persecution from others because he feels that the restraints come from alien sources and not from himself.

Projection is a very prevalent defense mechanism because from a very early age one is encouraged to look for the causes of one's behavior in the external world and discouraged from examining and analyzing his own motives. Moreover, a person learns that he can avoid punishment and self-blame by inventing plausible excuses and alibis for his misdeeds. He is, in effect, rewarded for distorting the truth.

There is another type of projection which may not seem, on first thought, to be defensive in character. It consists of sharing one's feelings and thoughts with the world. One feels happy and thinks that other people are also happy, or one feels miserable and thinks that the world is full of misery. Upon closer analysis the defensive nature of such shared projections becomes apparent. When other people are not happy one's own happiness is endangered, because it may make one feel guilty to be happy when others are unhappy. In order to remove that threat, one attributes happiness to others as well. If a person can convince himself that most people are dishonest, it makes it easier for him to be dishonest without feeling guilty. A student who habitually cheats during examinations often excuses himself on the grounds that nearly everyone else cheats, too. Or if he believes that sexual promiscuity is common he can use this belief to excuse his own sexual escapades. This type of projection does not involve the repression of the real motive and the substitution of another one. The person acknowledges that he possesses the motive but his moral anxiety is reduced by his projecting the motive onto others.

C. REACTION FORMATION   The instincts and their derivatives may be arranged as pairs of opposites: life versus death, love versus hate, construction versus destruction, action versus passivity, dominance versus submission, and so forth. When one of the instincts produces anxiety by exerting pressure upon the ego either directly or by way of the superego, the ego may try to sidetrack the offensive impulse by concentrating upon

its opposite. For example, if feelings of hate toward another person make one anxious, the ego can facilitate the flow of love in order to conceal the hostility. We might say that love is substituted for hate, but this is not true because the aggressive feelings still exist underneath the affectionate exterior. It would be more appropriate to say that love is a mask which hides hate. This mechanism whereby one instinct is hidden from awareness by its opposite is called *reaction formation*.

How can one differentiate between a simple cathexis for an object and a cathexis which is the product of a reaction formation? For example, what distinguishes love as a reaction formation from "true" love? The principal distinguishing feature of reactive love is that of exaggeration. Reactive love protests too much; it is overdone, extravagant, showy, and affected. It is counterfeit, and its falseness, like the overacting of the player-queen in Hamlet, is usually easily detected. Another feature of a reaction formation is its compulsiveness. A person who is defending himself against anxiety by means of a reaction formation cannot deviate from expressing the opposite of what he really feels. His love, for instance, is not flexible. It cannot adapt itself to changing circumstances as genuine emotions do; rather it must be constantly on display as if any failure to exhibit it would cause the contrary feeling to come to the surface.

A phobia is an example of a reaction formation. The person wants what he fears. He is not afraid of the object; he is afraid of the wish for the object. The reactive fear prevents the dreaded wish from being fulfilled. Reaction formations also stem from the superego; in fact the superego may be thought of as a system of reaction formations which has been developed in order to protect the ego from the id and from the external world. High ideals of virtue and goodness may be reaction formations against primitive object-cathexes rather than realistic values which are capable of being lived up to. Romantic notions of chastity and purity may mask crude sexual desires, altruism may hide selfishness, and piety may conceal sinfulness.

Reaction formations are employed against external threats as well as internal ones. A person who is afraid of another person may bend over backward to be friendly. Or a fear of society may take the form of strict obedience to the conventions of society. Whenever there is exaggerated and rigid conformity to any set of rules, one can be fairly certain that the conformity is a reaction formation, and that behind the mask of conformity the person is really driven by rebellion and antagonism.

An interesting example of a reaction formation is one displayed by men who are afraid of any sign of softness, which they equate with femininity, in their make-up. They try to cover up their feminine tendencies by being especially hard and masculine. As a result they become caricatures of masculinity rather than real men. Women may try to hide their femininity under a mantle of masculine attire and conduct.

Sometimes a reaction formation will satisfy the original wish which is being defended against. A mother who is afraid to admit that she resents her children may interfere so much in their lives, under the pretext of being concerned about their welfare and safety, that her overprotection is really a form of punishment.

Reaction formations are irrational adjustments to anxiety. They expend energy for deceptive and hypocritical purposes. They disort reality and they make the personality rigid and inflexible.

D. FIXATION

Although psychological development, like physical growth, is a gradual and continuous process during the first two decades of life, it is possible to distinguish rather well-defined stages through which a person progresses. For example, there are the four stages of infancy, childhood, adolescence, and adulthood. Normally a person passes from one stage to another in a fairly steady progression. Sometimes the progression comes to a halt and the person remains on one rung of the ladder of growth instead of taking the next step. When this happens in physical development we speak of the person's growth as having been stunted. When this happens in psychological growth we say that the person has become *fixated*.

Fixation is another defense against anxiety. The fixated person is afraid to take the next step because of the hazards and hardships that he sees lying ahead. Most children feel some apprehension when they start off for the first day at school, the adolescent is ordinarily not at ease on his first date, the high-school or college student looks forward with a mixture of worry and anticipation to his impending graduation, and practically everyone feels a little anxious when he undertakes a new venture of any kind. The anxiety that one experiences on leaving the old and familiar for the new and unfamiliar is called *separation anxiety*. When separation anxiety becomes too great, the person tends to remain fixated on an old way of life rather than advance to a new one.

What is the fixated person afraid of? What dangers interrupt the forward thrust of psychological development? The chief dangers are insecurity, failure, and punishment. Insecurity is a state of mind that develops when a person feels that he does not possess the ability to deal with the demands of a new situation. He feels that the new situation will be too much for him and that the outcome will be painful. Fear of failure is much the same sort of thing except that there is the additional fear of being ridiculed for failing. Failure is a blow to one's self-esteem (ego-ideal). Finally there is the fear of punishment, which may be the most important fear of all. Suppose a child is trying to assert his independence from his parents by developing interests and attachments outside of the family. That is, he is developing cathexes for other people and other things. He may be reluctant to make such object-choices because he is afraid that his parents will retaliate for his sharing his love with others by withdrawing their love, and that as a result he will be left alone and unprotected. At the same time he cannot be sure that the new object-choices will compensate for the loss of parental love. For the child or adolescent this may be a real dilemma, the outcome of which will determine whether he progresses or stands still. He is more likely to fixate if he has had previous experience with parental rejection.

It is ironical, but nonetheless true, that a child is more likely to be tied to his mother's apron strings by fear than by love. He is afraid of what she will do to him if he tries to assert his independence. A child who feels secure in his parents' affections and knows from experience that they will not reject him is not likely to become fixated on an immature stage of development.

In addition to fixation upon objects there are also fixations in the development of the structure and dynamics of personality. Some people do not advance beyond the level of wishful thinking. Others never learn to differentiate clearly between the subjective world and objective reality. Still others live under the domination of a severe superego or exist in a strait jacket of childhood fears. Some people fixate upon a particular defense mechanism around which their whole personality revolves. Others remain at the level of impulsive, discharge behavior. There are all kinds and degrees of fixation which prevent one from realizing his fullest psychological potentialities. Nearly everyone is stunted psychologically in some way by fear.

E. REGRESSION   Having reached a certain stage of development, a person may retreat to an earlier level because of fear. This is called *regression*. A young married woman who becomes anxious after her first quarrel with her husband may return to the security of her parents' home. A person who has been hurt by the world may shut himself up in a private dream world. Moral anxiety may cause a person to do something impulsive so that he will be punished as he was when he was a child. Any flight from controlled and realistic thinking constitutes a regression.

Even healthy, well-adjusted people make regressions from time to time in order to reduce anxiety, or, as they say, to blow off steam. They smoke, get drunk, eat too much, lose their tempers, bite their nails, pick their noses, break laws, talk baby talk, destroy property, masturbate, read mystery stories, go to the movies, engage in unusual sexual practices, chew gum and tobacco, dress up as children, drive fast and recklessly, believe in good and evil spirits, take naps, fight and kill one another, bet on the horses, daydream, rebel against or submit to authority, gamble, preen before the mirror, act out their impulses, pick on scapegoats, and do a thousand and one other childish things. Some of these regressions are so commonplace that they are taken to be signs of maturity. Actually they are all forms of regression used by adults. Dreaming is a beautiful example of regressive activity in that it involves the securing of pleasure by means of magical wish-fulfillment.

F. GENERAL CHARACTERISTICS OF THE DEFENSE MECHANISMS

The defense mechanisms of the ego are irrational ways of dealing with anxiety because they distort, hide, or deny reality and hinder psychological development. They tie up psychological energy which could be used for more effective ego activities. When a defense becomes very influential it dominates the ego and curtails its flexibility and adaptability. Finally, if the defenses fail to hold, the ego has nothing to fall back upon and is overwhelmed by anxiety. The result is a nervous breakdown.

Why then do defenses exist if they are so harmful in so many ways? The reason for their existence is a developmental one. The infantile ego is too weak to integrate and synthesize all of the demands that are made upon it. Ego defenses are adopted as protective measures. If the ego cannot reduce anxiety by rational means, it has to utilize such measures as denying the danger (repression), externalizing the danger (projection), hiding the danger (reaction formation), standing still (fixation), or retreating (regression). The infantile ego needs and uses all of these accessory mechanisms.

Why do they persist after they have served their purpose to the infantile ego? They persist when the ego fails to develop. But one reason why the ego fails to develop is that too much of its energy is tied up in its defenses. This is a vicious circle. The defenses cannot be given up because the ego is inadequate, and the ego remains inadequate as long as it depends upon the defenses. How can the ego break out of the circle? One important factor is maturation. The ego grows as a result of innate changes in the organism itself, notably changes in the nervous system. Under the impact of maturation, the ego is forced to develop.

Another important factor for healthy ego development is an environment which offers the child a succession of experiences that are synchronized with his capacities for adjustment. At no time should the dangers and hardships be so strong as to be incapacitating to the child or so weak as to be unstimulating. In infancy the hazards of existence should be small ones, in early childhood the threats should be a little stronger, and so on through the years of growth. In such a graded series of environments the ego would have an opportunity to shed its defense mechanisms (under ideal conditions they might never develop) and to replace them by more realistic and more efficient mechanisms.

IV. TRANSFORMATIONS OF THE INSTINCTS

The most striking difference between the baby and the adult, apart from physical differences in size and strength, is the contrast between the limited repertoire of behavior of the baby and the wide range of activities of the adult. A baby expends his energy in only a few ways while an adult has almost unlimited possibilities. How does energy find new channels for expressing itself? How does it come about that the fundamental instincts of life and death, which are the source of all psychic energy, branch out in all directions and provide the motive force for so many different kinds of adult transactions with the environment?

First, it is important to be clear about certain fundamental matters. The life and death instincts in the id originally contain all of the psychic energy. Psychic energy is produced by a transformation of bodily energy. The aim of the instincts is to remove bodily excitations and restore the person to a state of mental and physiological quiescence (freedom from tension). The instincts attempt to achieve this aim by using energy for psychological work, e.g., perceiving, remembering, and thinking. When the psychological work has been completed, that is, when a plan of action has been formulated, muscular energy is released in the form of motor action. The person does something. He talks, or walks, or uses his hands in order to bring about a desired result. The desired result is always a reduction of tension. This is achieved by removing the disturbing condition that produced the tension. Just how a mental plan of action is transformed into physical activity is not known. That it does happen must be obvious to everyone who has ever consciously thought of doing something and then done it.

When we ask why a person is doing something, whether it be collecting butterflies, washing his automobile, operating a lathe, or writing a book, what we want to know is what is motivating him. What particular instinct is directing his psychological processes in such a way that they lead him to collect butterflies, wash his automobile, operate a lathe, or write a book? We might think that there is a specific instinct for each one of these activities, but this hardly seems like a plausible explanation. At least it would not be a very economical one, and science strives for economy.

Rather we must look for the answer in what Freud called "the instincts and their vicissitudes." In one sense the answer to the question of how the restricted range of the child's behavior is expanded into the versatility of the adult's behavior would entail going back over everything we have already covered. A concise answer would be that the formation of the ego and the superego, the distribution of energy in the three systems and its utilization in cathexes and anti-cathexes, and the complicated network of interactions among the id, ego, and superego and all three with the world account for the increasing complexity of behavior.

Instead of repeating all that has been said, let us restrict our attention to a few important considerations. In the first place, few if any adult activities are the product of a single life or death instinct. Any particular action is more likely to be a consequence of a *fusion* of instincts. A person learns from experience that he can reduce tension arising simultaneously from a number of sources by engaging in a complicated activity. A football player, for example, is gratifying a number of instincts or their derivatives when he plays football.

Almost any activity is the condensation of a complex of motives. The fusion of instincts is accomplished by means of the synthesizing function of the ego. More of that later.

In the second place, an activity may represent a compromise between driving forces (cathexes) and resisting forces (anti-cathexes). As a result of resistances, the person cannot discharge tension directly; he must find some middle ground between complete satisfaction and complete dissatisfaction. For example, affection represents a compromise between the fulfillment of a sexual urge and ego resistances or superego prohibitions against such fulfillment. Likewise verbal criticism is halfway between physical aggression and non-aggression. The reason for the formation of compromises is found in the old saying, "Half a loaf is better than no bread at all."

Out of these displacements—for that is what compromise activities really are—new motives (object-cathexes) are acquired. When a person substitutes love for sex, it is said that he has formed a new motive. Actually, however, the new motive does not involve any change in the basic driving force or in the ultimate aim. The driving force is still supplied by the sex instinct, and the aim is still to remove the sexual tension. What changes is the means for achieving the aim. One tries to reduce sexual tension by desexualized expressions of love. These new motives or object-cathexes are called *instinct derivatives.*

Instinct derivatives are as numerous as the almost infinite number of displacements and compromises that man is capable of making. Attachments, preferences, interests, tastes, attitudes, habits, sentiments, values, and ideals are forms of instinct derivatives.

Compromise object-cathexes do not ordinarily discharge all of the tension. Romantic love, for instance, leaves a person with residual sexual excitation. An instinct that is prevented from discharging all of its energy is said to be *aim-inhibited*. Aim-inhibited instincts produce strong object-cathexes and persistent driving forces because they do not permit the complete discharge of tension. Consequently the undischarged excitations provide a continual stream of energy which is used to maintain the object-cathexes.

This leads to a seemingly paradoxical conclusion. Interests, attachments, and all the other forms of acquired motives endure because they are to some degree frustrating as well as satisfying. They persist because they fail to yield complete satisfaction. For example, a person who has an intense and insatiable interest in listening to classical music is not achieving full gratification. Listening to music is not a completely satisfactory substitute for a more basic object-choice. The music lover cannot get his fill of music because it is not really what he wants. Yet it is better than nothing.

Every compromise is at the same time a renunciation. A person gives up something that he really wants but cannot have, and accepts something second or third best that he can have. The lasting love of a child for its mother, and of the mother for the child, the good feeling that members of a club feel for one another, the love of one's country, and the multitude of other attachments that people form are all motivated by aim-inhibited instincts.

A third vicissitude undergone by the instincts is brought about by the action of the defense mechanisms. The defenses, it will be recalled, come into existence in order to help the ego deal with anxiety. Since one source of anxiety is danger from the instincts, the defense mechanisms try to avert the danger by altering instinctual object-choice. The death instinct, for example, is projected outward by the ego in the form of destruction, aggression, mastery, dominance, exploitation, and competition. This means that external objects are substituted for the original object-choice which is the person him-self. As long as the energy of the death instinct can be deflected away from one's own person, danger is averted and the person does not feel anxious. Here again we see the functioning of an aim-inhibited instinct. Inasmuch as action upon a substitute object can never be fully satisfying, projection of the death instinct will tend to persist. This accounts for the fact that aggressiveness is such a prominent human characteristic, and that the lesser forms of displaced aggression such as mastery, dominance, exploitation, and competition are even more prevalent. The weaker expressions are more prevalent than crude aggressiveness because they represent more of a compromise. Consequently, they are more persistently motivated because, failing to reduce as much tension, they have more available to maintain the habit. A fist fight is more satisfying (discharges more tension) than competition between business rivals, but adults engage in few fist fights and a great deal of competition. As a general rule, the more the substitute object-choice differs from the original one in providing relief from tension, the greater will be its hold over a person.

Repression of instinctual object-choices results in various kinds of substitute formations which serve to release energy in disguised forms. The disguise is accomplished by the substitution of one object-choice for another one. The purpose of the disguise is to prevent the ego from becoming anxious. As long as the substitute manages to fool the ego, and at the same time provides some reduction of tension, the substitute object-choice will persist. A person who has repressed his death instinct, for example, may get some satisfaction for his death wish by reading the death notices and obituary column in the newspaper, by attending funerals, and by listening to dirges. Better yet, he may become an undertaker.

Dreams are filled with disguised or symbolic representations of repressed desires. When the disguise becomes too transparent, the dreamer usually wakes up. Anxiety dreams and nightmares, for example, are caused by the emergence of repressed desires which makes the person anxious.

Reaction formation operates on the instincts not by substituting one object for another, as projection does, but by investing so much energy from one instinct in an object that it prevents the energy from another instinct from expressing itself. Modesty, for instance, may hide the desire to exhibit oneself.

In summary, all of the far-flung activities of the adult person are motivated by the energy of the life and death instincts. Anything that a person does is either (1) a direct expression of an instinct, in which case it would be a simple id object-choice like eating, sleeping, eliminating, and copulating, or (2) it is motivated by a combination of instincts, or (3) it represents a compromise between driving and resisting forces, or (4) it grows out of an ego defense.

We have neglected, however, to mention one other important kind of change that takes place in the instincts. Although the aim of the instincts remains constant throughout life, the source of the instincts, which is some form of bodily excitation, may change during the course of development. New bodily excitations arise, and old ones become modified or drop out as a consequence of maturation, exercise, stimulation, disease, fatigue, medication, diet, ageing, and interaction with other bodily excitations. These changes may add new instincts, eliminate old ones, or modify them in some way.

V. THE DEVELOPMENT OF THE SEXUAL INSTINCT

Freud's conception of the sexual instinct is much broader than the usual one. It includes not only the expenditure of energy for pleasurable activities involving genital stimulation and manipulation, but it also embraces the manipulation of other bodily zones for pleasure as well. A region of the body where irritating excitatory processes (tensions) tend to become focalized and whose tensions can be removed by some action upon the region, such as sucking or stroking, is called an *erogenous zone.* Manipulation of an erogenous zone is satisfying because it affords relief from irritation, as scratching relieves an itching sensation, and because it induces a pleasurable sensual feeling.

The three principal erogenous zones are the mouth, the anus, and the genital organs, although any part of the body surface may become an excitatory center demanding relief and providing pleasure. Each of the principal zones is associated with the satisfaction of a vital need, the mouth with eating, the anus with elimination, and the sex organs with reproduction. The pleasure derived from the erogenous zone may be and often is independent of the pleasure derived from the fulfillment of the vital need. For example, thumb-sucking and masturbation are tension-reducing, but the former does not satisfy hunger nor does the latter serve the cause of reproduction.

The erogenous zones are of great importance for the development of personality because they are the first important sources of irritating excitations with which the baby has to contend and they yield the first important experiences of pleasure. Moreover, actions involving the erogenous zones bring the child into conflict with his parents, and the resulting frustrations and anxieties stimulate the development of a large number of adaptations, displacements, defenses, transformations, compromises, and sublimations.

A. THE ORAL ZONE   The two chief sources of pleasure derived from the mouth are those of tactual stimulation, obtained by putting things in the mouth, and biting. Tactual stimulation of the lips and oral cavity by contact with and the incorporation of objects produces oral erotic (sexual) pleasure, and biting yields oral aggressive pleasure. Oral aggressive pleasure comes later in development because it has to await the development of teeth. If incorporation is painful, as it is when the baby takes in a bitter-tasting substance, baby gets rid of the offensive object by spitting it out. As a result of such experiences, the baby learns to avoid pain by shutting his mouth against irritating objects. On the other hand, if a pleasurable object is removed from the baby's mouth, for instance the mother's breast or the nursing bottle, the baby tends to hold on. The mouth, therefore, has at least five main modes of functioning, (1) taking in, (2) holding on, (3) biting, (4) spitting out, and (5) closing. Each of these modes is a *prototype* or the original model for certain personality traits.

By a prototype is meant an original mode of adjusting to a painful or disturbing state. It serves as a model for later adaptations. In other words, the child, having learned to make a particular adjustment, uses the same adjustment when similar situations arise later in life. If taking things in through the mouth is pleasurable, as it is when the child is hungry, then taking in or incorporating knowledge or love or power when one feels empty may also be pleasurable. In fact, we speak of a hunger for knowledge or love or power as though they were material things that could be eaten. The mouth provides many prototypic experiences which are transferred or displaced to other similar situations. Indeed, most of the prototypic experiences involve the body because the baby is more concerned with body functions than he is with the external environment.

Taking in through the mouth is the prototype for acquisitiveness, holding on for tenacity and determination, biting for destructiveness, spitting out for rejection and contemptuousness, and closing for refusal and negativism. Whether these traits will develop and become a part of one's character or not depends upon the amount of frustration and anxiety which is experienced in connection with the prototypic expression. For example, a baby who is weaned too abruptly may develop a strong tendency to hold on to things in order to forestall a repetition of the traumatic weaning experience.

By displacements and sublimations of various kinds, fixation upon one of the prototypic oral modes may develop into a whole network of interests, attitudes, and behaviors. A person who has acquired a predominantly incorporative orientation takes things in not only through the mouth but also through the sense organs, for example, by looking with the eyes and listening with the ears. The incorporative attitude may embrace abstract and symbolic things such as the incorporation of love, knowledge, money, power, and material possessions. Greediness and acquisitiveness develop as a result of not getting enough food or love during the early years of life. The acquisitive person is insatiable because whatever he is acquiring, whether it be money or fame, is only a substitute for that which he really wants, namely, food from a loving mother.

Because the baby is dependent upon an external agent, usually its mother, for relief from oral stress and the fulfillment of oral pleasures, the mother can control the baby's conduct by giving him the food when he is obedient to her wishes and withholding food when he is disobedient. Since the giving of food becomes associated with love and approval and withholding with rejection and disapproval, the baby becomes anxious when the mother rejects or leaves him, for this signifies the loss of desirable oral supplies. If a lot of anxiety is built up over this threat to the baby's oral pleasures, the baby tends to become overly dependent upon the mother and upon other people as well. He develops a dependent attitude toward the world. Instead of learning to satisfy his needs through his own efforts, he expects to have things given to him when he is good and taken away when he is bad. Such a person is said to have an oral-dependent character structure.

If the desire for dependence makes a person feel ashamed, a reaction formation may develop which will cause the person to resist being dependent upon anyone. He cannot ask anyone for anything because that would mean losing his independence.

Projection may also be used as a defense against dependency. Instead of seeking assistance, a person who projects will feel obliged to offer help to others. Such a person may take up nursing, social work, or some other humanitarian vocation. Or his repressed oral wishes may appear in disguised form. A person may become interested in linguistics, collect bottles, or learn ventriloquism.

Oral aggressiveness by biting is the prototype for many kinds of direct, displaced, and disguised aggressions. The child who bites with his teeth may as an adult bite with verbal sarcasm, scorn, and cynicism, or he may become a lawyer, politician, or editorial writer. We speak of "biting into something" or "taking the bit in one's teeth" when one displays aggressive, masterful, and dominant behavior. When one feels guilty, oral aggression may be used as a form of self-punishment. One may bite his lips or tongue.

Oral aggression may give rise to feelings of anxiety which are then defended against by various ego mechanisms. A person may react against oral aggression by saying only kind things about other people. Or he may project his oral aggression so that he sees himself as a victim of aggression from a world filled with enemies. He may become fixated on a primitive oral-aggressive stage of development (the oral biter) or regress to it when the frustrations of later stages are greater than he can handle.

Spitting out and closing up follow much the same line of development as taking in and biting. These prototypic modes of reaction are transformed in numerous ways, depending upon the particular satisfactions and frustrations that they encounter. The spitting-out type of personality is characterized by disdainfulness and contempt, the closing-up type by a shut-in, guarded quality. The erection of defenses against these modes of behavior as a result of anxiety affects the development of personality in many ways. For example, an undiscriminating acceptance of what anyone says or does, characterized by the expression, "He'll swallow anything," is a reaction formation against spitting out. A feeling of being a social outcast against whom the world has shut its door is a projection of shutting the mouth against a painful world.

The manifestations of these five modes of oral activity

may be seen in many theaters of life. They appear in one's interpersonal relations and attachments, in one's economic, social, political, and religious attitudes, and in one's cultural, aesthetic, recreational, athletic, and vocational interests and preferences.

B. THE ANAL ZONE   At the other end of the alimentary canal from the mouth is the posterior opening, the anus, through which the waste products of digestion are eliminated from the body. Tensions arise in this region as a result of the accumulation of fecal material. This material exerts pressure upon the walls of the colon, which is the part of the intestinal tract just behind the anus, and upon the anal sphincters, which are valve-like muscles. When the pressure upon the anal sphincters reaches a certain level, they open and the waste products are expelled by the act of defecation.

Expulsion brings relief to the person by removing the source of tension. As a consequence of experiencing pleasurable tension-reduction from elimination, this mode of action may be employed to get rid of tensions that arise in other parts of the body. Expulsive elimination is the prototype for emotional outbursts, temper tantrums, rages, and other primitive discharge reactions.

Ordinarily during the second year of life or earlier, the involuntary expulsive reflexes are brought under voluntary control through a set of experiences which is familiarly known as toilet training. Toilet training is usually the first crucial experience that the child has with discipline and external authority. Toilet training represents a conflict between an instinctual cathexis (the wish to defecate) and an external barrier. The consequences of this conflict are bound to leave indelible imprints upon the personality structure.

The methods employed by the mother in training the child, and her attitudes about such matters as defecation, cleanliness, control, and responsibility, determine in large measure the exact nature of the influence that toilet training will have upon personality and its development. A person naturally resists having a pleasurable activity interfered with and regulated. If the interference is very strict and punitive the child may retaliate by intentionally soiling himself. As he grows older such a child will get even with frustrating authority figures by being messy, irresponsible, disorderly, wasteful, and extravagant. Strict toilet-training procedures may also bring about a reaction formation against uncontrolled expulsiveness in the form of meticulous neatness, fastidiousness, compulsive orderliness, frugality, disgust, fear of dirt, strict budgeting of time and money, and other over-controlled behavior. Constipation is a common defense reaction against elimination.

On the other hand, if the mother pleads with the child to have a bowel movement and praises him extravagantly when he does, the child will come to regard the product he has made as being of great value. Later in life he may be motivated to produce or create things to please others or to please himself as he once made feces to please his mother. Generosity, giving presents, charity, and philanthropy may all be outgrowths of this basic experience.

If too much emphasis is placed upon the value of feces, the child may feel that he has lost something valuable when he defecates. He will respond to the loss by feeling depressed, depleted, and anxious. He will try to prevent future loss by refusing to give up his feces. If this mode fixates and generalizes, the person will be thrifty, parsimonious, and economical.

Retention or holding back the feces is the other mode of anal functioning. Although it may be employed as a defense against the loss of something that is considered to be valuable, retention is pleasurable in its own right. The gentle pressure on the internal walls of the rectum by the fecal material is sensually satisfying. Defecation terminates this pleasure and leaves one with a feeling of depletion and emptiness. If a person gets fixated upon this form of erotic pleasure it may develop into a generalized interest in collecting, possessing, and retaining objects.

A reaction formation against retention may develop

as a result of guilt feelings, in which case the person will feel impelled to give away his possessions and money in a heedless manner or lose them by making foolish investments or by reckless gambling. Having things makes such people so anxious that they will do almost anything to get rid of them. Moreover, they get some satisfaction out of spending their money in an expulsive manner.

C. THE SEXUAL ZONE   The third important pleasure zone of the body consists of the sex organs. Stroking and manipulating one's organs (masturbation) produces sensual pleasure. At the same time, there is an intensification of sexual longing in the child for the parents which initiates a series of important changes in his object-cathexes. The period of growth during which the child is preoccupied with his genitals is called the *phallic stage*.

Because the reproductive organs of the male and female are structurally different, it is necessary to discuss the events of the phallic stage for the two sexes separately.

1. *The Male Phallic Stage*   Prior to the emergence of the phallic period, the boy loves his mother and identifies with his father. When the sexual urge increases, the boy's love for his mother becomes more incestuous and as a result he becomes jealous of his rival, the father. This state of affairs in which the boy craves exclusive sexual possession of the mother and feels antagonistic toward the father is called the *Oedipus complex*. Oedipus was a prominent figure in Greek mythology who killed his father and married his mother. The development of the Oedipus complex creates a new danger for the boy. If he persists in feeling sexually attracted to the mother, he runs the risk of being physically harmed by the father. The specific fear which the boy harbors is that his father will remove the offending sex organ of the boy. This fear is called *castration anxiety*. The reality of castration is brought home to the boy when he sees the sexual anatomy of the girl, which is lacking the protruding genitals of the male. The girl appears castrated to the boy. "If that could

happen to her, it could also happen to me," is what he thinks. As a result of castration anxiety, the boy represses his incestuous desire for the mother and his hostility for the father, and the Oedipus complex disappears. Other factors also conspire to weaken the Oedipus complex. These are (1) the impossibility of fulfilling the sexual wish for the mother, as Oedipus did, (2) disappointments from the mother, and (3) maturation.

When the boy renounces the mother, he may either identify with the lost object, his mother, or intensify his identification with the father. Which of these will occur depends upon the relative strength of the masculine and feminine components in the constitutional make-up of the boy. Freud assumes that every person is constitutionally bisexual, which means that he inherits the tendencies of the opposite sex as well as those of his own sex. If the feminine tendencies of the boy are relatively strong he will tend to identify with his mother after the Oedipus complex disappears; if the masculine tendencies are stronger, identification with the father will be emphasized. Typically, there is always some identification as well as object-cathexis with both parents. By identifying with the father, the boy shares the father's cathexis for the mother. At the same time, the identification with the father takes the place of the boy's feminine cathexis for the father. By identifying with the mother, he obtains partial satisfaction for his sexual longing for the father, while the identification takes the place of the boy's cathexis for the mother. It is the relative strength and success of these identifications which determine the fate of the boy's character and his attachments, antagonisms, and degree of masculinity and femininity later in life. These identifications also give rise to the formation of the superego. The superego is said to be the heir of the Oedipus complex, because it takes the place of the Oedipus complex.

For a period of years, roughly between the ages of five, when the Oedipus complex is repressed by fear of castration, and twelve, when the energy of the sexual instinct is greatly augmented by physiological changes in the reproductive system, the sexual and aggressive impulses of the child are in a subdued state. This is called the *latency period*. With the onset of puberty, the impulses are revived and occasion the typical stresses and strains of adolescence. New adaptations and transformations take place during these adolescent years which culminate finally in the stabilizing of the personality.

2. *The Female Phallic Stage*   As with the boy, the girl's first love object, apart from the love of her own body (narcissism), is the mother, but unlike the case of the boy there is not likely to be an early identification with the father. When the girl discovers that she does not possess the noticeable external genitals of the male, she feels castrated. She blames her mother for this condition and the cathexis for the mother is thereby weakened. Moreover, the mother disappoints the girl in other respects. She feels that the mother is not giving her enough love or that she has to share the mother's love with brothers and sisters. As the cathexis for the mother weakens, the girl begins to prefer the father, who has the organ that she is missing. The girl's love for her father is mixed with envy because he possesses something that she does not have. This is known as *penis envy*. It is the feminine counterpart of the boy's castration anxiety. These two conditions, penis envy and castration fear, are aspects of the same general phenomenon, which is called the *castration complex*. The castration and Oedipus complexes are the two most important developments of the phallic stage.

The emergence of the castration complex in the boy is the principal reason why the Oedipus complex is abandoned, while in the girl the castration complex (penis envy) is responsible for the introduction of the Oedipus complex. She loves her father and is jealous of her mother. Although the female Oedipus complex is not as likely to disappear as the male's, it does become weaker by virtue of maturation and the impossibility of possessing the father. Identifications then take the place of object-cathexes.

Like the boy, the girl is also bisexual, and the strength of the identification with each parent is determined in part by the relative strength of the masculine and feminine predispositions of the girl. If the masculine component is strong, the girl will identify more with her father and become a tomboy. If the feminine impulses predominate, the girl will identify more closely with the mother. However, there is usually some degree of identification and cathexis with each parent. The girl's emulation of the mother brings her closer to the father and also compensates for the lost love relationship with the mother. Likewise, her identification with the father compensates to some extent for the missing genitals and preserves the cathexis for the mother. The strength and success of these identifications influence the nature of her attachments, hostilities, and the degree of masculinity and femininity in later life, as well as producing the superego.

The girl also has a latency period, when the impulses are under the domination of reaction formations. She emerges from latency at puberty. She, too, works through the problems of adolescence and finally achieves some measure of stability as an adult.

D. GENITAL SEXUALITY   The three stages of development, the oral, anal, and phallic, taken together are called the pregenital period. This period occupies the first five years of life. The outstanding characteristic of the sexual instinct during the pregenital period is its *narcissism*. This type of narcissism which is called primary should not be confused with so-called secondary narcissism. Secondary narcissism refers to feelings of pride which the ego experiences when it identifies with the ideals of the superego. Primary narcissism refers to the sensual feelings that arise from self-stimulation. Primary narcissism is body pleasure. It is exemplified by thumb-sucking, the expelling or retaining of the feces, and masturbation.

The sexual instinct during the pregenital period is not directed toward reproduction. The child cathects his own body because it is the source of considerable pleasure. He may also cathect his parents, but these cathexes develop because his parents, especially his mother, help him to achieve body pleasure. The mother's breast is the chief source of oral pleasure, and the caresses, kisses, and fondling of the baby by both parents are sensually satisfying.

Following the interruption by the latency period, the sexual instinct starts to develop in the direction of the biological aim of reproduction. The adolescent begins to be attracted to members of the opposite sex. This attraction eventually culminates in sexual union. This final phase of development is called the *genital stage*. The genital stage is characterized by object-choices rather than by narcissism. It is a period of socialization, group activities, marriage, establishing a home and raising a family, the development of a serious interest in vocational advancement and other adult responsibilities. It is the longest stage of the four, lasting from the late teens until senility sets in, at which time a person tends to regress to the pregenital period.

It should not be assumed, however, that the genital stage displaces the pregenital ones. Rather, the pregenital cathexes becomes fused with genital ones. Kissing, caressing, and other forms of love-making which are customarily indulged in as a part of the mating pattern satisfy pregenital impulses. Moreover, the displacements, sublimations, and other transformations of the pregenital cathexes become a part of the permanent character structure.

VI. SUMMARY

The development of personality takes place as a result of two major conditions. These are (1) maturation of natural growth and (2) learning to overcome frustrations, to avoid pain, resolve conflicts, and reduce anxiety.

Learning consists of forming identifications, sublimations, displacements, fusions, compromises, renunciations, compensations, and defenses. These mechanisms of personality all involve the substitution of new object-cathexes for instinctual object-choices. They also involve the formation of anti-cathexes which oppose the instinctual cathexes.

The formation of cathexes and anti-cathexes by the ego and superego, and the interaction between them, are responsible for the way in which the personality develops.

REFERENCES

Identification

FREUD, SIGMUND. (1921.) *Group Psychology and the Analysis of the Ego*, Chap. VII. London: The Hogarth Press, 1948.

FREUD, SIGMUND. (1923.) *The Ego and the Id*, Chap. III. London: The Hogarth Press, 1947.

FREUD, SIGMUND. (1923.) *New Introductory Lectures on Psychoanalysis*, Chap. 3. New York: W. W. Norton & Company, Inc., 1933.

Displacement and Sublimation

FREUD, SIGMUND. (1908.) "Character and Anal Erotism." In *Collected Papers*, Vol. II, pp. 45-50. London: The Hogarth Press, 1933.

FREUD, SIGMUND. (1908.) " 'Civilized' Sexual Morality and Modern Nervousness." In *Collected Papers*, Vol. II, pp. 76-99. London: The Hogarth Press, 1933.

FREUD, SIGMUND. (1908.) "The Relation of the Poet to Day-dreaming." In *Collected Papers*, Vol. IV, pp. 173-83. London: The Hogarth Press, 1946.

FREUD, SIGMUND. (1910.) *Leonardo da Vinci: A Study in Psychosexuality.* New York: Random House, Inc., 1947.

FREUD, SIGMUND. (1923.) *The Ego and the Id*, Chap. IV. London: The Hogarth Press, 1947.

FREUD, SIGMUND. (1930.) *Civilization and Its Discontents*, Chap. II. London: The Hogarth Press, 1930.

Defense Mechanisms

FREUD, SIGMUND. (1915.) "Repression." In *Collected Papers*, Vol. IV, pp. 84-97. London: The Hogarth Press, 1946.

FREUD, SIGMUND. (1921.) "Instincts and Their Vicissitudes." In *Collected Papers*, Vol. IV, pp. 60-83. London: The Hogarth Press, 1946.

FREUD, SIGMUND. (1936.) "A Disturbance of Memory on the Acropolis." In *Collected Papers*, Vol. V, pp. 302-12. London: The Hogarth Press, 1950.

FREUD, SIGMUND. (1937.) "Analysis Terminable and Interminable." In *Collected Papers*, Vol. V, pp. 316-57. London: The Hogarth Press, 1950.

FREUD, SIGMUND. (1939.) *Moses and Monotheism*, Part III, Sec. I, Chap. 5. New York: Alfred A. Knopf, Inc., 1947.

The Sexual Instinct

FREUD, SIGMUND. (1905.) "Three Contributions to the Theory of Sex." In *The Basic Writings of Sigmund Freud*, pp. 553-629. New York: Random House, Inc., 1938.

FREUD, SIGMUND. (1923.) "The Infantile Genital Organization of the Libido." In *Collected Papers*, Vol. II, pp. 244-49. London: The Hogarth Press. 1933.

FREUD, SIGMUND. (1925.) "The Passing of the Oedipus-Complex." In *Collected Papers*, Vol. II, pp. 269-76. London: The Hogarth Press, 1933.

FREUD, SIGMUND. (1925.) "Some Psychological Consequences of the Anatomical Distinction Between the Sexes." In *Collected Papers*, Vol. V, pp. 186-97. London: The Hogarth Press, 1950.

FREUD, SIGMUND. (1931.) "Female Sexuality." In *Collected Papers*, Vol. V, pp. 252-72. London: The Hogarth Press, 1950.

FREUD, SIGMUND. (1933.) *New Introductory Lectures on Psychoanalysis*, Chap. 5. New York: W. W. Norton & Company, Inc., 1933.

CHAPTER FIVE

The Stabilized Personality

The greatest changes in personality take place during the first two decades of life. This is the period in which a person is maturing and learning to overcome or adjust to external and internal frustrations and personal inadequacies, to acquire habits and skills and knowledge, to avoid pain and avert anxiety, to obtain goal objects and secure satisfaction, to compensate for losses, privations, and deprivations, and to resolve conflicts. By the end of this period, the personality has usually achieved some degree of constancy or equilibrium which persists until the deteriorative processes of old age set in. The organization and dynamics of personality are said to have become stabilized.

When we speak of the *stabilized personality* we do not mean to imply that all people develop the same pattern or even similar patterns of personality. There are many different kinds of stabilized personalities. Equilibrium may be established around a particular defense mechanism such as repression, projection, or reaction formation, or it may be based upon a particularly strong identification as happens when a person models himself after one of his parents or an older sibling or some other hero. Stability also results from the development of habitual displacements, sublimations, and compromises. The number of different patterns, displacements, and compromises is practically endless, as is evident when we contemplate the variety of adult activities. There are thousands of ways of occupying one's time. No two people have exactly the same patterns of interests, tastes, and attachments, yet each has arrived at a way of life which affords him some stability.

Nor do we mean by the term *stabilized personality* what others have called the mature, or wholesome, or well-adjusted, or ideal personality. These are all terms that may describe particular types of stabilized personality, but many people develop stability without ever becoming mature or well adjusted. Their stability may depend upon neurotic fixations and symptoms or upon psychotic withdrawals from the world of reality. The alcholic may be very settled in his ways, yet it could hardly be said of him that he is well adjusted. The oral dependent or anal retentive personality may have developed a high degree of consistency, but neither of these types is considered to be mature. Many stabilized personalities are actually stunted in their growth, for example, the perennial adolescent who never grows up.

Although the term *stabilized personality* may imply that the adult has settled down to a routine, humdrum existence, this is not the implication we wish to leave in the mind of the reader. Stabilization does not necessarily mean lack of variety in one's life, although for some people it may mean exactly that. Stabilization usually means that the variation will conform to a fairly consistent and predictable pattern. An adult may change his job or his wife or his hobbies quite frequently, but the new job or wife or hobby bears a close resemblance to the old one. Variations on the same theme (Freud's name for it is the *repetition compulsion*) rather than a succession of new themes characterize the behavior of the typical stabilized adult.

Finally, we do not mean by the stabilized personality one in which there are no frustrations, anxieties, or other kinds of tensions. Life is never free from tension. Rather, the stabilized personality is one in which more or less permanent arrangements for dealing with increases of tension have been made. What these arrangements are is the subject matter of the present chapter.

Clearly the most effective way to cope with or prevent

increases of tension is by utilizing the secondary process of the ego which, it will be recalled, consists of realistic thinking, reasoning, and problem solving. Given sufficient training and experience in rational, logical problem solving during the first twenty years of life and sufficient intellectual maturation, an adult should be able to solve most of the problems that confront him in a realistic and satisfying manner. In order for the secondary process to function efficiently it is necessary to check the object-cathexes of the id and the idealized cathexes of the superego by erecting anti-cathexes against them. Otherwise these cathexes will tend to distort the reality principle of the ego by contaminating it with wishful and moralistic thinking. Moreover, a continuous stream of energy must be made available to the psychological processes of perception, memory, judgment, and discrimination, since the secondary process makes abundant use of these functions.

The channeling of energy into ego processes means that the free energy of the id is converted into bound energy. Energy is said to be in a bound state when the freely mobile charge of energy which characterizes the instinctive excitations is transformed into a relatively quiescent tonic charge. This is accomplished by investing energy in the nondischarge functions of the ego. A person thinks instead of acts. An analogy may help to clarify what takes place when energy becomes bound. As long as a person has no financial obligations or responsibilities he can spend his money freely and impulsively. He can gamble it away or drink it up or spend it for whatever pleasures of the moment may attract him. However, when he assumes obligations by buying things on credit, by investing his money, or by paying taxes, or when he takes on the responsibility of providing regularly food, shelter, and the other necessities and comforts of life for himself and others, then he commits himself to spend his money for definite purposes. He has tied up his money in monthly bills and fixed expenses and can no longer spend it as he wants to. In just such a manner does the personality bind its psychic energy by investing it in stabilized and organized ego processes.

Stability is also achieved by investing energy in the mechanisms of projection, reaction formation, repression, fixation, and regression. If a person cannot deal with reality as it actually is, he can try to alter reality and make it consonant with his wishes or his ideals. Although these strategies on the part of the ego distort and falsify reality, they are effective nevertheless in affording protection from the disabling effects of anxiety and frustration. The stability afforded by the defense mechanisms may be a precarious one if the defenses are weak, but when one has had twenty years to strengthen the defenses they are not likely to crumble easily. The defenses drain energy from the secondary process and take the place of realistic thinking.

By the time a person has reached adulthood, displacements and sublimations have become established on a fairly permanent basis, and the transformation and fusion of instincts have been pretty largely completed. The experiences of the first twenty years have taught him how to make compromises which are to some extent satisfying or which, if not satisfying, at least help him to endure pain and anxiety. These compromises express themselves as interests, attitudes, attachments, and preferences. They have a hand not only in determining the major decisions of life—for example, the choice of a vocation and the selection of a mate—but they are also involved in the numerous minor decisions that have to be made in daily life. The consistency with which these choices are made and the so-called conservatism or resistance to change of the adult are due to the relatively fixed character of the adult's cathexes. The durability of these cathexes depends upon two important factors: (1) they are energized by a number of instinctual sources (instinctual fusion) and (2) they do not permit the complete discharge of tension because they are opposed by anti-cathexes. One's work, for example, involves a number of different activities which satisfy a variety of instinctual excitations, but the satisfaction of all the excitations at any one time is highly improbable. Ritual, tradition, custom, convention, uniformity, order, conservatism, habit, and repetition, all of which characterize the stabilized personality, represent compromises between driving forces (cathexes) and resisting forces (anti-cathexes).

This brings us to the role of the superego in adult personality. The cathexes of the ego-ideal represent sublimations of primitive object-cathexes. The character of the sublimations originally depends upon the kinds of behavior for which the child is rewarded. Whether a sublimation will persist or not depends, in turn, upon the satisfaction or the amelioration of pain that it continues to provide. If, in the long run, it provides no pleasure or amelioration, the sublimation will disappear. Accordingly, during the growing-up years, those ideals which are satisfying become entrenched and those which serve no purpose are sloughed off. The finished personality contains the residue of the idealized object-choices which are tension-reducing. Religious observances, community and welfare work, group participation, cultural, aesthetic, and literary pursuits, and nature study are representative adult sublimations.

In a similar way, the network of prohibitions (anti-cathexes) which is the conscience becomes stabilized. Prohibitions weaken and disappear when experience proves that the dangers upon which the prohibitions are based have vanished, while prohibitions which are periodically reinforced by fear of punishment become fixed in the personality. The ego is forced to come to terms with these superego anti-cathexes. It does so by finding some middle way between its own cathexes or those of the id and the anti-cathexes of conscience. This middle way is responsible for another common feature of the stabilized personality, namely, its moderation. There is ordinarily much less spontaneity and impulsiveness in adult behavior as compared with youthful behavior. However, should the anti-cathexes of the superego be very strong relative to the id or ego object-choices, the stabilized personality will be marked, not by moderation, but by rigidity. One who has such a personality lives a guarded, narrowly confined life. His stability is that of a person in a straitjacket.

In the final analysis, the stabilized personality is one that has achieved, through learning and maturation, a balance or equilibrium between cathexes and anti-cathexes. The nature of this balance, that is, whether it falls more on the side of fulfillment or more on the side of restraint or somewhere in the middle, is determined by the influences which are brought to bear upon the developing personality. A preponderance of prohibitions, threats, dangers, punishments, failures, deprivations, coercions, menaces, frustrations, inadequacies, and deficits will tend to erect and energize blocking forces within the personality; whereas a preponderance of successes, gratifications, victories, adequacies, and achievements will tend to favor the formation of cathexes. By and large, the presence of strong anti-cathexes will increase the tension level of personality since the anti-cathexes prevent psychic energy from being dissipated. However, in spite of the existence of considerable tension the personality can be quite stable as long as an equilibrium of forces is maintained. Some people who appear to be on the verge of flying to pieces momentarily retain their stability because the opposing forces are about evenly balanced.

Stability is also produced by the resolution of conflicts between opposing instinctual forces or their derivatives. The resolution of a conflict may come about in several ways. One of the contenders may win the upper hand over the other. For example, love may conquer or neutralize hate. This does not mean that hate disappears; it will continue to exist in a latent or suppressed form. Should love weaken, hate will again manifest itself. A conflict may also be resolved by finding ways of satisfying both of the conflicting motives. This may be accomplished by carrying on different transactions with different classes of objects. For example, one can display friendliness toward his associates (the in-group) and hostility toward strangers (the out-group). One can defe to superiors and bully inferiors. A conflict may also be resolved by alternately expressing one and then the other instinct upon the *same* object. Love can and often does take turns with antagonism in an intimate relationship. This form of resolution is like a needle that swings back and forth between two poles.

Probably the most prevalent way of resolving conflicts is that of fusion or integration. The person finds a way to satisfy both of the opposing forces in a single activity. For example, a person who holds a responsible position as a salaried employee in a large corporation satisfies both his desire for dependence, by being a salaried member of a secure and more or less paternalistic organization, and his desire for independence, by having duties and responsibilities which require independent judgment and initiative. Thus he is neither made too anxious by being overly dependent or too insecure by being completely independent. During the exploratory period of the first two decades, a person learns many ways of integrating his conflicts. He learns that he can have his cake and eat it too, although he can probably never have as much as he wants of either.

In summary, then, the stabilized personality is one in which the psychic energy has found more or less permanent and constant ways of expending itself in performing psychological work. The precise nature of this work is determined by the structural and dynamical characteristics of the id, ego, and superego, by the interactions between them, and by the developmental history of the id, ego, and superego.

REFERENCES

FREUD, SIGMUND. (1910.) *Leonardo da Vinci: A Study in Psychosexuality*. New York: Random House, Inc., 1947.

FREUD, SIGMUND. (1920.) *Beyond the Pleasure Principle*. London: The Hogarth Press, 1948.

FREUD, SIGMUND. (1930.) *Civilization and Its Discontents*. London: The Hogarth Press, 1930.

Recommended Readings

In addition to the writings of Sigmund Freud that are listed at the end of each chapter of the primer, the following list of books is recommended for the general reader. They are all written in a clear, interesting manner, and are, for the most part, nontechnical.

BARUCH, DOROTHY. *One Little Boy.* New York: Julian Press, Inc., 1952.

> If anyone doubts the crucial influence of sexual and aggressive feelings in the life of a young child, his doubts will be dispelled by reading this book. Written by a prominent child psychologist and therapist, it reads like a novel.

BERG, CHARLES. *Deep Analysis.* New York: W. W. Norton & Company, Inc., 1947.

> This book is an interesting sequel for *One Little Boy.* Dr. Berg describes, in some detail, the psychoanalysis of a man in his thirties. If one wants to know what happens during psychoanalysis as a method of treatment he will find it in this book.

BLUM, GERALD S. *Psychoanalytic Theories of Personality.* New York: McGraw-Hill Book Company, Inc., 1953.

> This useful and well-organized book presents a variety of viewpoints, Freudian, neo-Freudian, and non-Freudian. It is primarily concerned with the development of personality. Although written as a textbook it is not too technical for the general reader.

DEUTSCH, HELENE. *Psychology of Women.* 2 vols. New York: Grune and Stratton, Inc., 1944.

> There is very little that this famous woman psychoanalyst does not know and tell about her sex. It is a fascinating study of feminine psychology.

ERIKSON, E. H. *Childhood and Society.* New York: W. W. Norton & Company, Inc., 1950.

> An outstanding child psychoanalyst shows how the ego of the child develops in relation to society. He illustrates his main points by the use of excellent case material taken from his own experiences.

FENICHEL, OTTO. *The Psychoanalytic Theory of Neurosis.*
New York: W. W. Norton & Company, Inc., 1945.

This comprehensive account of Freud's abnormal psychology is
considered to be authoritative and definitive. The meatiness of
this book makes it somewhat difficult to read, but it is well worth
the effort.

HENDRICK, IVES. *Facts and Theories of Psychoanalysis.*
New York: Alfred A. Knopf, Inc., 1947.

Dr. Hendrick, a well-known American psychoanalyst, writes with
authority and clarity about all aspects of psychoanalysis.

HORNEY, KAREN. *New Ways in Psychoanalysis.* New
York: W. W. Norton & Company, Inc., 1939.

Dr. Horney is known as a neo-Freudian (one who accepts some
of Freud's concepts while rejecting or revising others). It is said
of Horney that she adopts a more sociological viewpoint than
Freud did. Some readers may find her views more palatable than
those of Freud.

JONES, ERNEST. *The Life and Work of Sigmund Freud,*
Vol. I. New York: Basic Books, Inc., 1953.

The first volume of a projected three-volume work covers the
formative years and the basic psychological discoveries of Sigmund Freud. This biography has been characterized as one of the
great biographies of modern times. The reader who is interested
in the life and work of Freud might well begin his reading with
this excellent work by the distinguished British psychoanalyst.

MENNINGER, KARL. *Man Against Himself.* New York:
Harcourt, Brace and Company, 1938.

Dr. Menninger, the Topeka psychoanalyst, has written a detailed
and documented account of the death instinct.

MULLAHY, PATRICK. *Oedipus Myth and Complex.* New
York: Hermitage House, 1949.

This compendium includes just about everything one would want
to know about the Oedipus complex, which Freud considered to
be one of his most important discoveries.

STERBA, RICHARD. *Introduction to the Psychoanalytic
Theory of the Libido.* New York: Nervous and Mental
Disease Monographs, 1942.

A brief, lucid account of Freud's theory of the development and
vicissitudes of the sexual instinct.

INDEX

125

Other MENTOR and SIGNET Books
of Special Interest

☐ **PSYCHOANALYSIS AND PERSONALITY by Joseph Nuttin.** The noted Belgian psychologist discusses the relation between modern depth psychology and Christian philosophy. Revised edition. (#MY950—$1.25)

☐ **THE UNDISCOVERED SELF by C. G. Jung.** A solution to man's conflicts and problems through a deeper understanding of one's inner self is discussed by the renowned psychiatrist. (#MQ1051—95¢)

☐ **GESTALT PSYCHOLOGY by Wolfgang Kohler.** A classic statement of the basic concepts of a psychological theory which has profoundly influenced the progress and direction of modern psychology. (#MY1302—$1.25)

☐ **PASSIONS OF THE MIND by Irving Stone.** Irving Stone's brilliant retelling of the life of Sigmund Freud captures the Vienna of the 1880's, the gay and brilliant capital of Europe, where Freud began his long struggle to free men from the chains of their unknown natures. (#J4953—$1.95)

THE NEW AMERICAN LIBRARY, INC.,
P.O. Box 999, Bergenfield, New Jersey 07621

Please send me the MENTOR and SIGNET BOOKS I have checked above. I am enclosing $_____(check or money order—no currency or C.O.D.'s). Please include the list price plus 25¢ a copy to cover handling and mailing costs. (Prices and numbers are subject to change without notice.)

Name_____

Address_____

City_____State_____Zip Code_____
Allow at least 3 weeks for delivery